# ES
# Thinking

## EXTRAORDINARY LIVING THROUGH EGO SPIRIT THINKING

## SUSAN KREBS

little pink press™

*ES Thinking*

Cover design: Keryl Pesce

Author photo: J. Ferrara Photography

Published by Little Pink Press, P.O. Box 847, Beacon, NY 12508

ISBN: 1-7329494-3-3
ISBN-13: 978-1-7329494-3-0

# Dedication

To my son Kyle:

From even before you were conceived, I loved you.
Since the moment I held you, you gave me a reason to heal.
You were the catalyst that helped me dig deep
and be the next best version of myself.

Always remember our motto:
"Through good and bad…
We'll get through it together!"

# Contents

# Acknowledgments

With Deepest Gratitude to:

Mary Demetria Davis, my friend and Spiritual Coach. I can't even put into words my gratitude for all you have taught me over the past twenty years. Your unwavering support, unconditional love, unending patience, vast knowledge, and incredible connection to spirit have been my guiding lights. This book could not have been written without you! I love you!

Kyle, my first and only born! My heart bursts with love for you! I am honored to be your mom and am grateful each and every day you are my son. You are evolving into this incredible man/boy, and I am in awe of your big heart and kind spirit. You have supported me even when you did not understand what I was doing. Thank you for all your love!

Mom, my first teacher. You taught me about God, how to be kind and were always my most fierce cheerleader. You encouraged me to be the best mother I can be. You continue to support me and love me unconditionally, and for that I thank you. I love you so much.

Dad, who taught me about the importance of never giving up on someone. I love you so much and cherish all our good memories. I am grateful for your lessons on how beautiful nature is and how God sustains us through any trial and tribulation, including death. I feel your love and support just as much, if not more, since you have transitioned on. Thank you for all your guidance from the other side.

Marion, my sister. You have been the best big sister I could have ever asked for. Your love, patience, and calm, laid-back personality has been a Godsend to me. You never once blinked an eye when, out of the blue, I told you I was writing a book. You have cheered me on through every step and believed in me. You have taught me so much—way more than you will ever know. I love you and am so blessed to be a part of your soul pod!

Jimmy, my brother. You are and always have been a tower of strength for me. I know having an annoying little sister was a trial at times, but whenever I needed you, you have ALWAYS been there, no questions asked. Our relationship has given me many opportunities to grow and learn about the importance of loving myself, and I am grateful for all your love and support. I love you!

Lauren, my sister-in-law. Wow did our family hit the jackpot when you came into our world! Your peaceful, grounding presence had been so calming whenever I have felt amid a raging storm. Our talks have been enlightening, and you have been paramount in helping me connect with my body in a loving way through your nutrition and exercise coaching. I love you so much!

Madison and Mackenzie, my nieces. Two beautiful souls who have lit up my world. I am the most blessed aunt EVER! I adore both of you. You each have your own unique personality, and you both have hearts of gold, a sense of humor that cracks me up, and a love for family that is precious to me. I am so excited to be a part of your lives and love you both so much.

*ES Thinking*

My Aunt Cathleen and Aunt Maureen. You both have taught me the importance of family and traditions. I can only hope my nieces think I'm half as cool and fun as I think you two are! I love you both!

My cousin Kathleen. We have been best friends for forty-eight years! I can't thank you enough for all the HOURS and HOURS that you have listened to me go through my process. You are a saint, for goodness sake, AND you still totally love me! LOL! I am honored to be on this path with you! You continually blow me away at how open you are to explore new ways to grow. You challenge me to be open when I want to close up and call me on my shit when I need it the most! I would not be where I am today without you! I love you so much!

My dearest friend, Carla Barbano (owner of A Dog's Life Camp and Spa). Your friendship has had such a profound effect on me. You have been my confidante for more than twenty years. In your no-nonsense way, you help to push me out of my comfort zone to learn new things and believe in myself. You introduced me to Mary Demetria Davis, and you have gifted me my last two dogs, who have given me years of unconditional love and joy. You have my deepest gratitude for all your advice, love, and care that you bestowed upon Sammy and now with Bodhi. You give with all your heart, and I am blessed to be your friend on this journey. I love you!

My core, Christine Rauschenbach and Suzanne DeGroat. Our connection and unconditional love for each other has gotten me through the scariest parenting moments with our gift of gab and laughter. You were the first people outside of my

iii

healing circle of friends and family to whom I opened up about my spirituality and visions for this book. Your unconditional acceptance of all parts of me gave me the courage to stand up and be seen. I love you both!

My friend Jen Rose. Our weekend morning coffee klatch has been a treasure to me. Your unconditional love and support have kept me sane! I will always cherish our mutual love of dogs and Sammy and Buddy's friendship. You are a gift from God, and I love you!

My Violet Alchemy (VA) Family Circle. My deepest gratitude to Ama'zjhi/Dona Ho Lightsey. She is the creator of Violet Alchemy® Healing, Purification, and Empowerment. Calling you my spiritual teacher seems small in comparison to what you have done for me. Introducing me to Violet Alchemy® helped me to heal and release so many layers of old wounds and strengthened my connection to spirit in such a deeper way.

My VA sisters and brothers were and continue to be a huge support to me on my healing journey. A shout out to Cat Santoro, Alissa Jane Lepska, Kristin Ryan, Molly Tweedy, Jonathan Hornig, Lisa Jones (Millionaire Medium), Luke Kohen (Aloka), and Stephanie Santagada. Love you guys!

To my VA sister, Donna Brickwood, of Sacred Space. You have shared a wealth of information with me throughout this whole book-writing process and have helped me overcome many blocks, not just with this book, but in my ever-evolving process. I love you, girl!

To Saint John's Youth Ministry —LoriAnn and Anthony O'Brien, Denise Alhgrim, Susan White, Patty Ferlauto, Henry

Melchiona, Sue Cartier, Laura Frodell, Marie Schindlar, Brian Schnurman, Glenn Elmen, and Kevin Sherman (to name just a few)! Also, in memory of and deep gratitude to Noel Ruiz and Joe Campanello~ forever in my heart. In my early teens, I was at a crossroads. Your friendship, love, and support were God's guiding light for me, leading me down the road to unconditional love. I am forever grateful for each and every one of you.

To Keryl Pesce. You believed in my vision and made it happen. Your creative talent and ability to get right to the heart of the message was so appreciated. You are another beacon of light for me sent straight from God.

To Bonnie Hearn Hill. So grateful for all your expertise! You are another critical piece to making this book a reality. Divine timing was at its best when you had a small window of time open just when I needed a top-notch editor!

I could go on and on...trust me. Just ask anyone who knows me! There are so many people who have impacted me in some way that I am grateful for. In my heart, I am sending out waves of gratitude to each one of you. You know who you are, and if you don't, your soul does. The light in me honors the light in you!

# Foreword

I am the Co-Director of the Princeton Center for NLP (Neuro-Linguistic Programming) and have been a life coach for more than thirty years. I drew upon twenty years of prior business experience, extensive NLP training, and a multitude of other certifications to develop strategies that would help people to live with more ease and joy. In addition to my work experience and education, the one constant on my journey was my spiritual approach to living.

When Susan and I met, she was looking for a coach to help her navigate through a few issues. My job was to facilitate and introduce ways for her to communicate more effectively with others but, most importantly, with herself. We remained curious as we explored how to validate feelings without judgment in a variety of contexts.

Susan was definitely a seeker and eager to learn, and both of us shared a spiritual connection and loved taking notes. We were a perfect fit. Little did we know that our notes would grow into a book.

We created strategies/recipes utilizing bits and pieces of techniques and modalities to improve or accomplish our outcomes. In addition, we'd focus on the use of language in a particular context, understanding that "It's not what you say but how you say it." I'd come up with recipes, and being a learner and a curious being, Susan had the capacity and motivation to test them out.

We started to see that there was a common thread that surfaced when we did work, regardless of the context. We became aware of how our ego identity served us and had a positive intent but in fact, sometimes got in our way and kept us stuck. We also became aware of how our spirit identity was alive and well, waiting for us to ask for help. We identified the need to balance the ego and the spirit and adopted the term "ES Thinking."

This is Susan's story. She is sharing her personal journey with you and telling you how ES Thinking was "the difference that made a difference" for her. Our collaboration over the years resulted in clarifying her experiences as they relate to the exercises that are presented in this book.

ES thinking is a choice, when you are aware of their presence and honor both parts of ego and spirit. Our spirit loves us unconditionally and knows our capabilities; it's that place of inner wisdom. Spirit is working when so often you have those "Wow! Where'd that come from?" moments. In this book, you will learn how to communicate and tap into the best of the best of you more effectively when ego and spirit are working together for your highest good. You'll learn what ES principals to use when you want to maintain more harmony and peace in your daily living. I am honored to invite you to take what fits for you and explore how ES Thinking can enhance the quality of your overall life too.

-Mary Demetria Davis

# Introduction

"An identity would seem to be arrived at
by the way in which the person faces and
uses his experience."

~ James Baldwin

My intention for writing this book is to share with you
the steps I took in my journey and how I was able to overcome so many challenges by choosing love. My hope is that
you can benefit from it as well.

Living in today's world is, in my opinion, a roller coaster
of movement and emotion. It is full of moments that are
reaped with a full range of feelings. From feeling in awe of
mind-blowing beauty, to utter despair and every possibility in
between, we experience them all. What I have discovered,
and perhaps you have too, is that time can sometimes be a bit

of an illusion. Have you ever experienced something that was so amazing, that made you so happy and full of joy that you wished it would last forever? And before you knew it, the experience had passed, in the snap of a finger. Or what about the opposite end of the spectrum, when you feel depressed, stuck, wishing the time would pass quickly? The same amount of time can seem like forever. What is all this about?

In the uncomfortable times of uncertainty and struggle, have you ever asked yourself any of the following questions: How am I going to get through this? Will I ever find peace again? Happiness again? How do I manage myself among all this turmoil? How do I manifest all I want and desire with so much uncertainty in life? Does it get ANY better? Is there really such a thing as a light at the end of the tunnel?—'cause, honey, it sure looks dark and scary to me!

These are just a sampling of some of the thoughts and questions I have asked myself during the challenging times in my life. Lucky for me, a beautiful and brilliant person named Mary Demetria Davis was introduced to me as a Life Coach. What I have learned by working with her has been a game changer for me. My ability to choose perspectives and re-sponses that overwhelmingly move me toward the kind of person I want to be and living the kind of life I desire is im-measurably better than before she came into my life. I have also changed the way I feel about myself, and I am blown away by the difference. I owe her more than words can ex-press. And I owe it to you to share what I have learned, so you too can be aware that no matter what comes your way, you know the best choice to make… the one that reinforces your confidence in yourself and what the future holds.

As my spiritual journey ensued, and I grew in joy, love, and confidence, clear and identifiable patterns emerged, steps that others could follow. The patterns emerged, and Ego Spirit Thinking was born. It became clear to both Mary and me that we had to spread the word and share the lessons we learned. We had to bring to others that which has the capacity to forever alter the course of their lives for the better. What follows is a collection of strategies that have been tried over and over again in many different contexts. Ultimately, I learned how to use my ego and spirit to work together to help manage the daily challenges of living. You've likely been told you are supposed to transcend the ego, do away with it, and overcome it. How can you expect to banish something that is inherently a part of being human? Of being you? I don't think that is the objective. The objective is to incorporate the positive aspects of our ego, to use it to our benefit, rather than fight it. And you do that when you choose love. Always. Unconditionally. I hope I have presented what lies in the pages ahead in such a way that it gives you more peace of mind as you navigate through the inevitable ups and downs of life.

Today, my level of understanding of human nature and my ability to release, forgive, heal, and transform my life has grown by leaps and bounds.

Once I started choosing love, my life as I knew it was no more (in a really good way)! Doing so has lifted me to places that have allowed me to manifest all my dreams and then some! Had you told me four years ago that I would be changing careers and writing a book, I would have laughed out loud and said you were crazy! Like REALLY CRAZY! Believe me, if I could do it, you can too.

As you read more about my journey and what I discovered along the way, take for yourself what feels right for you. The beauty is that you get to choose what fits and use it! Or not. And that's okay.

Although not easy, I felt it was important for me to share some of the details of my life and how I came to be where I am today. Years ago, I would have lacked the courage to do so, but I have learned, and I hope you do as well, that the details of our story are not our identity—they are just a part of the human experiences we have. And while they do not define us, they certainly do shape us. The beautiful thing is how they shape us is our choice. Everything I have experienced has assisted my heart and spirit to evolve and to develop a higher understanding of my human journey as a spiritual being. And I am grateful for every bit of it.

We each have our own unique story made up of human experiences that have occurred in our lives. One is not to be compared to another. Pain is pain, regardless of how it was inflicted. Shame and guilt are real emotions we all experience, regardless of how they came to be. It is important to understand that there is a distinction: our story happened to us, but it is not our identity. How we grow and learn and expand, given our unique life experiences, is how we define who we are. We don't always get to choose what happens to us, but we always get to choose what to do with it. Here's to the power of choice. Here's to choosing love.

# I

## The Story That Shaped Me

"Don't forget, you are the hero of your own story."

~Greg Boyle

Since as long as I can remember, people fascinated me. By studying the people around me, I learned how I thought a person should act, be, and feel. It was very important to me for people to like me and think that I was a "good girl." If everyone thought that, then I must be doing it right.

Growing up in a household with an unpredictable and sometimes violent alcoholic father and an angry and over-whelmed mother was very stressful to say the least. Especially for this little girl who was trying to make sure everyone liked her and was happy. To make matters worse, I was sexually abused by a neighbor, from as young as two years of age until thirteen years old. These environments, with the help of my ego, taught me many life lessons and helped to formulate limiting beliefs that would impact how I lived my life and dissociated from pain and challenges. Here are some examples:

- ~ I learned what fear was.
- ~ I learned what instability felt like.
- ~ I learned that my needs were secondary to achieving peace; brief moments of security and peace were easier to obtain if my needs did not matter.
- ~ I learned how vital it was to keep secrets and bury the shame and guilt associated with them.
- ~ I learned to have a distorted view of my body.
- ~ I learned a distorted view of what love was.
- ~ I learned that my behavior made a difference; if I acted in a certain way, it could cause turmoil, but if I acted in a different way, I could make the people around me happy, and that made me happier.
- ~ I learned that I must do anything I could to survive and feel brief moments of happiness.
- ~ I believed that I was responsible for keeping the peace and making others happy.
- ~ I learned ways to diffuse the tension by acting in certain ways with certain people.

Although it may seem hard to believe at times, our ego is actually looking out for us. It wants us, and it, to survive. In order to cope, I learned from a very early age to take on roles in order to manage the people around me *and* this thing called life. It was an overwhelming responsibility, and this sense of responsibility stayed with me through my twenties, thirties, and even the beginning of my forties. These lessons and limiting beliefs saw me through two divorces. They taught me how to survive some harsh situations. I am grateful for my ego because I did survive. I did well in school and went to college. I got my master's degree and was completely independent, working as a successful speech pathologist by age twenty-three, and later, even getting through two divorces and being a single mom. Survival is the motivation behind our ego.

The ego is just one important part. My spirit also played a role in my survival.

I grew up going to church every Sunday in a Roman Catholic Church, believing that God was this outside source I must please. At age thirteen, I became involved in my church's youth group and sang in the folk group. It gave me the sense of family I was starving for. On one weekend retreat, I remember telling a priest about how I was abused. Unfortunately, he likely had a host of his own traumas and basically told me to forget it ever happened and to never speak of it again. The shame deepened, and I felt God was not happy I had broken the unwritten code of silence.

As I got older, I transferred to a Presbyterian Church and then periodically went to an Episcopalian Church. While each church taught me many valuable lessons, I was still searching for the meaning of God in a way that resonated with me and made me feel as if I were home. I then started studying Buddhism and the Tao. I began meditating and learning about the art of different modalities of energy healing. I adopted the motto, "Take what pieces fit and leave the rest." In essence, my spiritual practice is not at all religious in nature, but instead, made up of various tools that have cultivated a belief that there is a higher power leading me on a journey of unconditional love for myself and others.

I would have to say that one of my most defining moments in changing the course of my life occurred after having The Dream. Until that point, I was stuck in a continuous loop of "Why do bad things happen?", "Why can't my life be easier?", "Why does everything good seem so hard to achieve **and** maintain?", "Why can I get there briefly but can't seem to stay there?" I understood my ego self and my spirit. I even understood when I was in one energy or the other. The difficult part was the "why" questions. I had a hard time letting go of the past and the emotions attached to my life experiences up to that point. I was still easily stuck in the victim mentality. One evening while I was questioning all of this, I felt the need to mediate. My meditation sometimes leads to falling asleep (which I refer to as "beditating"), and during this beditation, the following vision/dream came to me:

> I was walking with a group of people to a place where there was an incredibly fun ride. I say people, but we were not in the human form. It was more like we were each individual bundles of light and energy. A friend was guiding us to the place where we were to take off. It is difficult to put into words the high level of excitement that we all felt at being given the opportunity to go on this ride. Our energy bodies were zinging with excitement! I knew this ride because I had been here before.
>
> One by one, when we got to the top of the hill, we climbed onto a sled. When we were ready, we got a push off, and away we went! It was amazing because there was no snow. It was more like a roller

coaster. I went around curves, up and down dips and hills, and it was truly exhilarating. At the end, it came to a stop, and I got off by a building, where I saw people milling about and admiring the incredible views. I meandered around and looked out across a beautiful lake at the most incredible sunset.

The next thing I knew, I was inside the building, and I knew I did not have long to live on this plane. With this realization, all the ego attitudes and beliefs just fell away. I was rooted in the frequency of love. I stayed in the building with the amazing knowledge of what life was really about. Different people would come in and sit to hear me talk about my experience. I realized at one point I only had one month to live, and I was radiating from a place of pure love. At that point, I lost my eyesight, but it did not matter because my spirit was vibrating at such a high level of love. I asked for help freely and without hesitation whenever I needed it. People were asking me, "How much time do you have left?" and my response was, "It doesn't matter. Time is an illusion, and all that matters is this moment right now and the joy we can bring each other!" I was so happy. It was pure, unbridled joy!

I spoke with people I had never met before, and then family members came in. It was a celebration of my life. My mom was standing across and to my left but as a younger version of herself. She was more like an apparition. My cousin was in the back by the door, talking to people, and then my sister-in-law came in. She walked over to me, and as we hugged, I started to cry. I was reflecting on how these three people represented the trinity in my human experience. My cousin was my mind, my sister-in-law was my body, and my mom was my spirit. My three parts! My cousin and I have been best friends since childhood, and she has listened to me hour after hour (and hour and hour) as I moved through my spiritual journey. My sister-in-law has been my nutritional coach and Pilates instructor off and on through the years and instrumental in my connection to my body, and my mom helped start me on my spiritual journey. I was crying because I knew I was transitioning soon, and I was going to miss being human. This was so powerful.

The main message was the feeling of vibrating from a place of love, releasing all the attitudes of anger, rage, shame, guilt, need for protection, fear, and judgment. Just raising my frequency to love was all I needed to do. In the vision, it was so easy (not so easy in the human form... just saying).

When I woke, a message came clearly to me. When we decide to reincarnate, we are so excited. We feel like it is a gift to be given the opportunity to live as a spiritual being having a human existence. As we were sent off on our ride, that was the human birthing process. We actually choose to be human to heal past wounds and move toward a greater understanding and enlightenment of what it truly means to be in the energy of love. We are honored and excited to be human **even knowing the trials that await us**. We are so blessed to be on this path... we just forget this when we become human... we tend to get caught up in the illusions our ego brings up to help us survive pain.

In that moment, it became clear: what's done is done.
The past is the past, and I have two choices.  I can choose to
look at my life from a place of ego, and with it, all the anger,
rage, shame, guilt, need for protection, fear and judgment that
came from my life experiences.  Or I can choose to look at
those experiences from that vibration of love from my heart
space. This enables me to see the lessons I have learned and
continue to learn, moving on to a place of understanding,
forgiveness, strength, and acceptance, which leads to growth
and love.

> "In any given moment we have two options:
> to step forward into growth or
> to step back into safety."
>
> ~ Abraham Harold Maslow

Let's explore the meaning of love.  If we look at the
scripture from 1 Corinthians 13; 4-5, "Love is patient, love is
kind, it does not envy, it does not boast, it is not proud, it
does not dishonor others, it is not self-seeking, it is not easily
angered, it keeps no records of wrongs." It is a safe unconditional God love; it is the highest form of God love.  This is
the vibration that serves our spirit and ego.

**What do you choose?**

Because we all have the freedom of choice, why not
choose this definition of love, that supports the balance between our ego and heart space?  Most of us default to living

life rehashing old wounds and seeing them repeat themselves in the current day. Turn back around, BE HERE NOW and create the tomorrow you desire and deserve from that place of love. If you're constantly looking back at what was, it's like walking into your future backward and missing the present, the gift of this moment, this day. How you think has an impact on how you feel, and how you feel drives your behavior.

I invite you to change your perception of pain and hardship! By doing so, you can move forward from a place of love, having more understanding and strength as you deal with day-to-day life.

The challenge is to choose that safe, unconditional highest form of love (God love). You won't regret it!

# 2

## Is It Just Me?

"The ego is a tool. You don't separate it.
It is a tool for the spirit."

~Ram Dass

The answer is "NO." There are two essential parts of us that CAN work together: Ego and Spirit. The ego and the spirit working together is key. Communication between the two is essential. Making time to connect and look at the roles of each and how they impact each other is vital for the relationship to survive. Once an alignment and balance are created between the two, you will be able to achieve peace of mind with more ease and frequency. That is what living from an ES center is all about.

## DEFINITIONS (from dictionary.com):

### EGO:
~ A person's sense of self-esteem and self-importance.
~ The part of the mind that mediates between the conscious and the unconscious and is responsible for reality testing and a sense of personal identity.

### SPIRIT:
~ The nonphysical part of a person that is the seat of emotions and character; the soul.
~ The nonphysical part of a person that is regarded as the person's true self and as capable of surviving physical death or separation.

### PEACE of MIND:
~ Freedom of disturbance; quiet and tranquility.
~ Mental calm, serenity.

As soon as we can connect with each part, we become more aware of how we do us. Once we become more aware of how we do us, we can start to build a relationship between the two, valuing both parts and creating a relationship where we can improve and move forward on our path of understanding and enlightenment, while having a human experience.

Here are some differences between the identities of our ego and spirit:

| EGO | SPIRIT |
|---|---|
| Conscious Mind | Subconscious Mind |
| Reasoning/Beliefs and Values | Intuition and Inner Knowing |
| Fears/Doubts | Faith/Trust |
| Judgments/Questions | Allowance/Acceptance |
| Give up and revert to survival reactions | Let go for a moment and react with peace and love |

### Who's dominant?

When ego takes on a more dominant role, the tip of the scale creates an unbalance. If ego is the driver in the ES relationship, we are allowing fear, anxiety, and lack to dictate how we react each day. For example, if you are a person who struggles with finances or the feeling of not having enough, ego thinking steps in to help. It's that small voice that can be critical, bring up doubts, and make you question your self-worth. Coming from this place, we are only bringing in more of that.

Believe it or not, there is a positive intent behind that behavior! Ego is driven by the desire to make sure we survive in whatever situation we find ourselves. It will use whatever method necessary to help us "get through" the situation regardless of the consequences. That critical ego voice we hear is trying to get us to go out and get more money! "Hurry up, you're going to be late again on your payments! You are always overspending! You need lots of money, and then it will be all right!" Ego thinks that by using criticism, it is motivating us!

On the other hand, if we allow spirit to be the driver, we are allowing love to drive our reactions, and we will bring in more love. Think of the money scenario. If we are looking at it from our heart center, we are our own personal cheerleader: "You got this! You always figure out a way to make it, and another solution will make itself known!" That sounds a lot more motivating to me than what our ego was saying!

Some might ask, "Why not just get rid of the ego? It has no benefit." It is my belief that having an ego is what defines us as being human. You may have heard of the saying, "We are spiritual beings having a human experience." Our ego is not going anywhere as long as we are existing as humans. Its purpose is to help us survive and protect us from pain. It is a beautiful, essential part of our human existence. Our experiences are made up of duality: good/bad; pain/pleasure; hate/love; yin/yang. Ego/spirit is another example of that duality. We would not be able to know what love is without experiencing its counterpart. It's the same with ego and spirit. Without the ego, we would not be able to fully appreciate our spirit because we couldn't experience the dichotomy that exists between the two. This defeats the learning and whole purpose of being human. Part of our life lesson is to recognize the ego, learn how to validate its positive intent, and using that information, move into a position where our spirit can lead us through day-to-day living from a place of love.

Ego directs our attention to what is outside of us and has an impact on the way we regard ourselves. Do we look good, do we have the right car? Spirit directs our attention inward to a place that loves us unconditionally, no matter what.

This safe, unconditional highest form of love is what our reason for being here is all about. We each have a roadmap of what our life lessons and purpose are. We are not here in this human form just to exist. There is so much more going on here then getting a job or developing that career, getting married, or having kids, retiring, and then dying. From a human perspective, all that sounds well and good, but from a spiritual perspective, there is more! The ultimate goal and human purpose is to come into alignment with your soul: alignment from a place of unconditional love of self **and** others. How we get there is ruled by freedom of choice and how we react to contrasts that come up in our lives each day.

If you believe in a higher power, source energy, universe, spirit, God, Buddha, etc., that gives you UNLIMITED opportunities to move toward greater understanding that improves our human life from a place of unconditional love. And if you don't believe in those, you may be more open to the concept that we each have a spirit, our heart center, soul, or core, working for our highest good. For the purpose of this book, I will be using the terms higher power/God/spirit interchangeably while referencing the above concepts.

Our reason for being born into this human form is to embrace the limitations that ego gives us and learn to be a co-creator with our spirit, living with more understanding and enlightenment of this path of life. It is to heal old karmic wounds and break past agreements and cycles that have interfered with our moving toward higher understanding and enlightenment.

What a gift it is to be human! The journey is ever changing and the knowledge that we can acquire is UNLIMITED.

FEAR, ANGER, CRITICISM, JUDGMENT, SHAME, BLAME, REVENGE, are all **gifts** that ego gives us to use as an opportunity to heal. That's why learning how our ego plays its role in having this human experience we call LIFE is so important. Many may wonder how those qualities of the ego can be considered a gift. Remember when I challenged you to change your perception of pain? Well, this is part of that. As we begin this journey of recognizing our feelings and actions of our ego, the potential is there to learn how to feel and act DIFFERENTLY. That is the gift.

In order to heal our feelings, we must first acknowledge them, validate them, and get to know what those feelings look like, feel like, and sound like. As we recognize them when they come up in everyday life, we become more aware of the destructive patterns associated with them and realize we now have a choice in how we want to react.

The same is true for the feelings of UNCONDITIONAL LOVE, ACCEPTANCE, and BEAUTY IN ALL FORMS. Once we take time to get to know what that looks like, feels like, and sounds like, we start recognizing them when they come up. We then become aware of the safe, secure, accepting, and freeing patterns that emerge and change our lives for the better, even amid chaos.

Moving back and forth between ego and spirit and learning how to shift into "Spirit Thinking" is the key to living our human experience from a more centered and balanced perspective. As we learn to shift into our connection to our spirit, the more self-love and acceptance we will experience.

The more we feel it, the more we want to learn how to receive and give it.

This is moving forward on our path to a greater understanding and sense of peace and enlightenment while receiving all the beauty and love life has to offer us. It is being in the world but not of it: it's all good.

There are many steps during this process and many facets to each step to explore. I encourage you to take the time to get to know how you do you. YOU'RE WORTH IT!

This is an introspective journey and will be unique in many ways for each of us. It is tailored specifically to your individual life lessons and purpose. **But, the overall theme and steps of how we get there is universal.**

**CHOOSE LOVE.**

# 3

## Let's Explore Our Ego and Spirit

"Realize that you are already whole, complete, perfect,
and loved. You are both Ego and Spirit.
Affirm your wholeness."

~unknown

### Ego

When we talk about the ego identity, it is important to
remember that the ego is vital to our spiritual development.
We have defined it as a person's sense of self-esteem and self-
importance. It is the part of the mind that mediates between
the conscious and the unconscious, and it is responsible for
reality testing and a sense of personal identity, that is, who we
are.

We start developing our ego at birth, and its primary job is to help us survive and avoid pain. It's the part of us that takes in information from our surroundings and gives us feedback on what we need to do in order to grow and live in our world.

Remember that fear, anger, criticism, judgment, shame, blame, and revenge, are all **gifts** that ego gives us to use as an opportunity to heal and learn. We need the contrast that ego gives us in order to discern who we are, where we want to go, and how we want to be. This awareness helps us to recognize destructive patterns that are associated with the ego. That's why learning about our ego and how it plays its role in this human experience we call LIFE is so important.

The following is a list of big issues that plague many of us in today's world. Take a moment to think about your life as you read through them.

- You or your family members or friends are having a health crisis or health concerns.
- You're working in a toxic work environment or in a job that is not fulfilling.
- You're in an unhappy or abusive relationship.
- You're worried for your children as they go through their own struggles.
- You're suffering with an addiction.
- You're having financial struggles and do not have enough money to pay bills.
- You have so much stress or anxiety that just getting through the day is difficult.
- You have a long commute and feel like there is never enough time.

- ~ You do not have enough time to be the parent you want to be.
- ~ You're juggling children's schedules with your own.
- ~ You lack the time and energy to help out that friend or family member.

It is easy to get caught up in a situation that is challenging us and to default to fear. Fear then triggers criticism, judgment, anxiety, shame, blame, or the desire for revenge. Life can be harsh at times, but we end up only hurting ourselves more when we get stuck in these patterns of ego thinking. That is why the balance between our ego and heart/spirit is vital. That balance supports us in remaining centered and grounded in the ups and downs of daily life.

When I started to identify when I was in my ego state, I decided to have some fun with it! So, let's just say when that car cut me off, and there was no one behind me, I immediately defaulted to my ego state and said some nasty things to that driver! When a colleague of mine asked a question they wouldn't have had to ask if they'd read the email I sent, the initial response in my head was definitely driven by my ego state! Or when my kid was acting out in public, and I was mortified, I'll admit I was surprised I could have such negative thoughts about the child I birthed into this world! Or when that "friend" gave me a compliment that we both knew was a backhanded criticism—BAM—in my head, was ego state extraordinaire!

It was easier at first to identify my ego state when it was in relation to an outside person or situation. Only after I practiced more did I realize how often I was in my ego state with regard to myself. I started noticing how often I put myself down with negative self-talk. Here are some examples:

*God Sue, you just opened your mouth and inserted your foot horribly.*

*What were you thinking by doing that?*

*Why did you eat that? You're never going to lose weight. Look at yourself! Who is ever going to be attracted to that body?*

*OMG, you are a horrible mother. You should have never overreacted like that!*

*You're so stupid!*

*You deserve to die if you won't quit smoking!*

*You are a financial FAILURE!*

In fact, I began to realize that I had dialogues going on in my head throughout the entire day! Not all was negative, but much of it was. It was a huge eye opener. I was my own worst critic. If someone else spoke to me that way, I would want to punch them! OK, maybe not punch, but I would want to be done with them. I knew I was critical of myself but did not realize the extent of it until I became more aware of how my ego operated my thoughts. I began understanding my ego had a positive intent even though it had negative consequences. This was just the beginning.

Below is an exercise to help assist you in identifying when you are in your ego state. Being able to identify when you are operating from that state is critical in starting the process. Take some time to answer the following questions and fill in what applies to your experience. There is not a right or wrong answer. I invite you to be curious and honor whatever comes up for you.

$$\infty$$

## Ego Exploration:

### How do you identify with your ego?

Think of a couple of different situations that have brought up emotions of fear, criticism, judgment, shame, blame, or the need for revenge. It can be directed at yourself or others.

What does your ego look like, feel like, sound like?

☐ Do you see a picture in your mind?

_____

_____

_____


☐ Is it in black and white or color?

_____

_____

_____

☐ What colors do you see?

_____

_____

_____

☐ What emotions come up?

_____

_____

_____

☐ Do you feel it any specific place in your body?

_____

_____

_____

☐ Is it pressure or pain?

_____

_____

_____

☐ Does it have a shape?

_____

_____

_____

☐ Do you feel heat or get flushed? Describe the experience.

_____

_____

_____


☐ Do you hear a voice inside of your head or outside of you?

_____

_____

_____


☐ What is that voice saying? Are you hearing any particular sound (i.e. sound of a train, high-pitched sound)?

_____

_____

_____


☐ What is the tone of the voice or sound?

_____

_____

_____


☐ If you hear a voice, is it yours?

_____

_____

_____

**What feelings are evoked when you are connected to your ego?**

☐  For each of the above experiences, what emotions are connected to it?

_____

_____

_____

_____

_____

☐  What is the positive intent of your ego?

_____

_____

_____

Remember that our ego's intent is not to hurt us. Its motivation is to help us survive and has a positive intent behind every thought and action. Some examples of positive intent could be:

~  To protect us from harm or pain.

~  To stop us from repeating a negative action.

~  It could be that it does not want us to feel discomfort by looking too deeply at our own responsibility in a situation. It is easier and less painful to focus on the actions of others or go into denial.

~   To motivate us to do things differently.

The goal of this exercise is to help you identify when you are in your ego state. When you find yourself looking back on a part of your day, look for situations when you were in your ego state and think about how you know that. Think of the above questions and what clued you in. Eventually, the more you do this, the more you will find yourself being able to immediately identify when you are reacting or being driven by ego.

Remember we are all in our ego state at various points throughout the day. Some more than others! This is **NOT** a judgment! I am encouraging you to accept yourself exactly as you are! Our ego is vital to our development and serves its purpose to give us the contrast we need to learn and grow! Thank your ego for all it does to help you survive in this crazy world we live in!

**Spirit**

Our spirit is just as vital to our development as the ego is. This is the other part of us that is made up of love. We define it as the nonphysical part of a person that is the seat of emotions and character; the soul. It is regarded as the person's true self and as capable of surviving physical death or separation. It has also been referred to as our higher self.

You're connected to your heart space in your spirit when you are experiencing feelings of unconditional love, acceptance, and beauty in all forms. Once we take time to get to know what that looks like, feels like, and sounds like, we can recognize them when they come up. We become aware of the safe, secure, accepting, and freeing patterns that emerge and change our lives.

Personally, this part was easier for me to identify with versus the ego state. My meditation practice has assisted me greatly in quieting my mind and going inward, connecting with and feeling unconditional love and acceptance. It was interesting to me, though, to learn how I was connected to my spirit in ways throughout the day that I didn't even acknowledge or realize. I began noticing **"moments."**

~ When I held my son in my arms and rocked him to sleep.
~ When an incredible sunset caught me off guard.
~ When I experienced that beautiful scene in nature that I wanted to stay in forever.
~ When I looked into one of my difficult students' eyes and really saw that child as a loving being, deserving of love.
~ When I stopped my car and let an older woman cross the street. It was that moment when our eyes connected, and she smiled with gratitude.
~ When I was sitting around laughing with girlfriends, and for a moment, I just looked around at each of them so grateful for them in my life.
~ When I realized I was completely in my anxiety-driven OCD state, talking nonstop, and my sister just let me go on without judging me.
~ When I was in grief, crying, and I looked down to see my dog's head on my lap, just holding loving space for me to let go.
~ When I realized that inward place I would go to in meditation was fully accessible anytime. In that mo-

ment, taking a breath and using it to ground me was all I needed.

These moments are so powerfully loving that I naturally want to create more of them. The amazing thing is that we have the power to create these moments for ourselves anytime we want. We can start by living with more awareness.

∞

**Spirit Exploration:**

**How do you identify with your spirit?**

Think of a couple of different situations that have brought up emotions of unconditional love and acceptance. Think of a time you have been awestruck by something beautiful. It can involve just you or a place, person, or thing.

What does your spirit look like, feel like, sound like?

☐ Do you see a picture in your mind?

_____

_____

_____

☐ Is it in black and white or color?

_____

_____

_____

☐ What colors do you see?

_____

_____

_____

☐ What details come up?

_____

_____

_____

☐ Does it have a shape?

_____

_____

_____

☐ Do you feel it anyplace in your body?

_____

_____

_____

☐ What emotions come up?

_____

_____

_____

☐ Describe the experience.

_____

_____

_____


☐ Do you hear a voice inside of your head or outside of you?

_____

_____

_____


☐ What is that voice saying?

_____

_____

_____


☐ Are you hearing any particular sounds?

_____

_____

_____


☐ What is the tone of the voice or sound?

_____

_____

_____

☐ If you hear a voice, is it yours?

_____

_____

_____

## What feelings are evoked when you are connected to your spirit?

☐ For each of the above experiences, what emotions are connected to them?

_____

_____

_____

_____

_____

## What is the positive intent of your spirit?

☐ This answer is uniquely individual. If you're having trouble answering this question, just write down the first thing that comes to mind.

_____

_____

_____

_____

_____

The goal of this exercise is to help you identify when you are connected to your spirit. When you find yourself looking back on a part of your day, look for situations where you were connected to your spirit and think about how you know that. Think of the above questions and what clued you in. Eventually, the more you do this, the more you will be able to immediately identify when your spirit is leading.

This is the exciting part! Now you are becoming aware of when you are in your ego or spirit state.

# 4

# An Overview of ES (Ego Spirit) Thinking

"What is necessary to change a person is to
change his awareness of himself."

~Maslow

Have you ever said, "Why did I do that?" This question
has the potential to be a turning point. Awareness is the key
in building a relationship between your ego and your spirit,
valuing and utilizing both parts with ES Thinking and living.

## What is Ego Spirit (ES) Thinking?

ES Thinking is the process of building a relationship between our ego and spirit in such a way that supports our life
with more peace and joy. By recognizing that the two can co-

exist, this will support our highest good in any situation. ES Thinking requires us to explore and take time to embrace both ego and spirit.

ES Thinking is the key to living a centered, more balanced life despite the darkness and struggles that present themselves in your daily life.

ES Thinking takes courage and time to embrace yourself totally with more insight, love, and appreciation.

As we become **aware** and identify the positive intent behind our thoughts and behaviors, we begin to understand there are consequences for such behaviors, both good and bad. We have a choice.

In a negative situation, most people will have a knee-jerk reaction from ego state. That includes judgment of self and/or others. Ego reaction is often based in fear/doubts expressed in emotions. Spirit reaction is acceptance with faith and trust without judgment.

When using this thinking process, we are living differently. We are more open to unlimited possibilities and resources for good in our lives. Using ES Thinking will give us insight as to HOW to survive living in today's world from a place of light when darkness **SEEMS** so prevalent.

> "This is when we are in it, but not of it…
> whatever the "it" is."

Think of a time where you were at work or home, and people were in a disagreement that created a very negative environment. Many people feel very uncomfortable or get pulled into those situations, even if it has nothing to do with them.  Is it ours to participate in?  Or not?  If it is ours, ES Thinking helps us address the issues and communicate more effectively without the negative emotional charge.  If it is not, then we are able to walk away or refuse to get involved.

Have you ever tried to change a behavior that you knew was not serving you? Welcome to the club. Let's say we want to start exercising.  People tend to start out strong and then after a period, give up.  We may let life get in the way.  How does that make you feel? What do you say to yourself to help motivate or justify your behavior?  Your ego is dominant if your thoughts and feelings are negative, and you find yourself beating yourself up.  We tend to be our own worst critics.  ES Thinking occurs when you give yourself time to explore your thoughts and feelings without judgment.  Once you start validating and releasing limiting beliefs, thoughts, and feelings, you are giving yourself the opportunity to view this same situation with love. The outcome can't help but be different in some way.

These are examples of how both ego and spirit are working coherently, creating more positive thoughts and behavioral patterns.  We are in it but not of it.

Attitude has such an important impact on how you manage life each day.  Think about it. How you think triggers certain emotions, and those emotions drive your behaviors. This is what attitude is all about.  Think of a time you have been around someone who has a negative attitude. What effect did it have on you? What effect does it have on you when you are around someone with a positive attitude?  Attitude has an energy associated with it.  It impacts your tone of voice, the way you hold your body, and how you feel.  It can be contagious!  Attitude is triggered by how you perceive your thoughts and situations. Are you aware of the thoughts you wake up with? What's your intention for the day? How you think will have a direct impact on how you feel. What thoughts and emotions are you waking up with? If you wake up on the wrong side of the bed, get back in bed and start again. By the way, I have totally done this!

"This is the day the Lord has made, let us rejoice and be glad." We have a choice. Let's turn those lemons into lemonade. Sometimes that's easier said than done because many times, we wake up with the worries of yesterday and the "should've, could've, or would've" mentality that is driven by our ego state identity. We can't change what has already happened and we can't control how people around us are going to act.

> "We have a choice every day regarding the attitude we will embrace for the day. Life is 10% what happens to us and 90% how we react to it. Our attitude is everything."
>
> ~Charles R. Swindoll

We can choose to start our days on a positive note. By embracing our spirit identity, we are recognizing that it's a new day, with the intent of making it as peaceful as possible.

When ego is connected to the heart/spirit, we are living life from an ES center. Life, when lived from the heart, supports our being in balance. When we're living from an ES center, it has a positive effect on others. We start managing and reacting out of love for ourselves and others. Even in conflict where we can agree to disagree, the overall energy is

42

still more positive.

We are building a collective consciousness of the highest form of love. We are a pebble making a rippling effect.

# 5

## The Importance of the Now Moment

"All negativity is caused by an accumulation of
psychological time denial of the present. Unease, anxiety,
tension, stress, worry—all forms of fear—are caused by too
much future, and not enough presence. Guilt, regret, resentment, grievances, sadness, bitterness, and all forms of
non-forgiveness are caused by too much past,
and not enough presence."

~Eckhart Tolle

ES Thinking has three essential parts: thoughts, emotions, and behaviors. Our mind is our ego that controls that
voice in our head that talks to us throughout our day. The
more you consciously connect with your ego/mind, the more
aware you are of your emotions. Those emotions are trig-

gered by your thoughts, and you begin to see how emotions drive your behaviors. This awareness is the essence of ES Thinking.

Have you ever consciously connected with your thoughts? I mean really listened to them. Our society today is so filled with external stimulation visually and auditorily that it is easy to drown out our thoughts and become desensitized to them. For many of us, our thoughts are non-stop loops that go on in our heads throughout the entire day. Experts have estimated that we think **at least** 50,000 thoughts per day which is the equivalent of 2,100 thoughts per hour. Good grief, that is crazy when you think of it that way!

Eckhart Tolle talks about how thinking has become a disease. He states in *The Power of Now* that disease happens when things get out of balance. Your mind is an amazing instrument that can help you achieve a higher understanding of yourself. It can also become destructive if you let it be in the driver's seat and lead you throughout your day. Many of us mistakenly believe our minds are who we are—and we are so much more. Your mind is that ego part that can become out of balance when it doesn't connect with your spirit. This is why it is important to develop a relationship between the two so they can work together.

I'm a talker, and I can talk A LOT. I tend to process life verbally by talking about whatever I am thinking. My ex-husband used to tell me, "You couldn't pay me to spend a day in your head. You never stop, and it is exhausting!" At first, I did not know what he was referring to, but as I started to connect with my thoughts, I realized how right he was! I was exhausted by my own thinking!

The first step is awareness, and to achieve it, you need to bring yourself into the present moment of what your thoughts are. Eckhart Tolle calls it "watching the thinker," and I resonated strongly with this concept. I began to sit back and remove myself from my thoughts. Up to that point, I really did think I WAS my thoughts, and my thoughts were me. It was one of those defining moments in my journey— the moment I understood that I was NOT my thoughts and that I could sit back and observe them. I realized that while they were a part of how I did me, they were not my full identity. They did not define who I was. I had the power to change them. That realization was a game-changer! In that moment, when I stepped back to observe my thoughts, I shifted into my spirit. The journey was just beginning.

Think of a time when you were going through your day, and you thought of something that made you internally giggle or laugh out loud. In that brief moment, you were an observer of your thoughts. Or maybe when you thought of something really nasty and critical of someone else and you thought to yourself, "Wow, that is seriously not right!" You might feel bad and shift into another thought. That is you observing your thoughts and experiencing your feelings that are connected to those thoughts.

Once you are consciously aware of observing your thoughts, you are separate from them. That separateness you experience allows you to connect with your body and your spirit. How connected are you to your body? More often than not, people today are so focused on external factors, that they have forgotten what it is like to "just be." Our world today is very chaotic, full of stress and mental anguish, and at times, we feel like we are on a never-ending treadmill without a stop button. Sure, we receive some messages our body gives us. We feel tired, so we have more caffeine. We have indigestion, so we take antacids. And for that headache, there's always aspirin. To "just be" means getting off that treadmill. It means stopping what you're doing for just a moment. Connecting to your body and your breath is being fully present in the moment of Now.

Lorie Ladd is a beautiful soul who has dedicated her life to providing practical teachings to help people shift into higher states of consciousness. In one of her videos, she speaks about how we all have energy that moves throughout our body. To me, she is describing our spirit. Our spirit is this vibrating energy field that is housed within our physical body. By bringing ourselves into this Now moment, we are connecting to this vibrational frequency. By focusing on our breath, we can connect to the energy of our spirit.

## Now Moment Exploration (from Lorie Ladd):

Close your eyes, take a deep breath, and let it out completely. Do this a couple of times.

- □ As you release your breath, gently move into your body and feel what your body is feeling.
- □ Are your feet touching the ground, do you feel the chair or bed underneath you?
- □ Are you holding tension anywhere in your body?
- □ Are feeling relaxed?
- □ Do you feel the flow of energy moving through your body?
- □ What does all this feel like?

It may feel different during different points in the day or activity. Honor whatever experience you are having. Let go of any labels or judgments of what you think it should be like.

Remain curious.

Everything around you is still going on. Life's problems and worries are still present externally. In **this moment**, you are connected to your body and spirit in a safe way. You're breathing with more ease and allowing thoughts to come and go until you're not thinking, just being fully present in the Now.

You can also do this during mindless tasks during the day, while outside walking, setting the table, or doing laundry. I was given the exercise once of being fully present while I was washing dishes. As I did this, I had to give every aspect of the act my full undivided attention. I observed the feeling of water on my hands, the temperature, the way the sponge felt as it moved over each dish. I listened to the sounds of the water changing with each step. I connected with my body and how I was breathing, how the mat felt under my feet, how my clothes felt on my body.

It was difficult at first, and honestly, I kept initially "thinking" *what is the purpose of this? This is not doing a thing for me!* Then, I realized how my thinking kept interfering with the moment, and I kept practicing. I practiced it while I was taking a walk, as I was falling asleep in my bed at night, and then one day, I finally got it! As I was practicing, I began connecting with this indescribable feeling of peace. It was only moments at first, but then I started to feel it more and more and understood that in that moment, all was right in my world. There was no past, no future, just this incredibly beautiful, loving moment of me connected to my body and spirit. I wanted more!

# SUSAN KREBS

.

# 6

## Criticism and Judgment Zone vs. Free Zone

## The Choice Is Yours

"The world exists as you perceive it.
It is not what you see, it is how you see it.
It is not what you hear, it is how you hear it.
It is not what you feel, but how you feel it."

~Rumi

There are a couple of critical keys that we need to be aware of as we set the foundation for our new way of thinking from our ES center.

At all times, our thoughts are either in a criticism and judgment zone or a free zone. When we are thinking critical thoughts of ourselves or others, we are obviously in the criticism and judgment zone. When we are thinking neutral or loving thoughts, we are in the free zone connected to spirit.

Inherently, we are conditioned from birth to avoid pain. When a child is crying, we want to immediately find out what they need and provide it for them. When we don't feel well, there is a plethora of over the counter medications and prescription drugs to alleviate the symptoms. Look at how huge lotto is; we are trained that if we only had money, our problems and the pain associated with financial woes would be eradicated. Some people—if their hearts have been broken in a relationship—have to jump right into another relationship to make the pain and loneliness go away. If only we had that new car or the latest phone or the biggest house, we would be happy. Look at the suicide rate; that is very telling. People today are not equipped with the skills needed in order to feel, release, and heal their pain. Our society has been brainwashed to believe that an "outside force" will make us feel better. If we feel good, then we don't feel the pain. It's a Band-Aid!

Don't get me wrong. It's perfectly normal to want to feel good. That is my goal every day. Who wouldn't want to live in Utopia? The part that is important to distinguish here is that in our human existence, it is impossible **not** to have pain. Pain is a part of every human's teachings.

> "ES thinking is not avoiding and putting a
> Band-Aid on pain, but addressing it."

Addressing pain is scary as hell! I get it. I resisted it for years and should have purchased stock in Band-Aids. Only when I realized that I was perpetuating the cycle of pain in different forms did I choose to do it differently. Was it easy? No way! I am not going to lie to you; sometimes it really hurt. Did it change my life? OMG... yes! I found the courage to experience the pain that I spent years hiding from. The sense of freedom and liberation I felt after letting it out was exhilarating at times. I had no idea how exhausting it was to try to keep it buried. Seeing the pain for what it truly was, validating, and managing it, ultimately led to my healing and growing from that pain.

We start this journey by recognizing what zone we hang out in. As I started to become aware of when and how often I was in my ego state, I was blown away with how much I was in my criticism and judgment zone. At this point in my life, I had years of counseling to help me come to terms with the hurt and pain associated with my childhood experiences. I thought I was "healed" and had moved on from the trauma. I began to realize how my ego was still trying to prevent any of that pain from happening to me as an adult. That was the positive intent behind my critical and judgmental attitude of myself, others, and situations.

Ego kept me in the critical and judgmental zone that fed fear, anger, resentment, shame, and guilt. Unfortunately, it kept me stuck in the negative emotions through my internal dialogue justifying how it was keeping me safe. It was a vicious cycle.

As I increased my awareness, I began to realize how negatively I spoke to myself. Here's just a sample of my internal dialogue. I heard it all loud and clear.

~ *I told you people can't be trusted.*
~ *If you want something done right, you have to do it yourself.*
~ *Don't trust him; men use you for their own gain.*
~ *Work is always going to be like this. Just get used to it.*
~ *You should be grateful you have a job.*
~ *Money doesn't grow on trees, and you always overspend.*
~ *What are you going to do next month when you're short?*

Criticism and judgment are detrimental to our growth and inhibit our ability to attain more understanding and enlightenment. The more aware we are of when and how we criticize and judge ourselves and others, the more we can choose to shift our thoughts into our free zone. The more we reside in our free zone, the easier it is to live in our truth from a place of unconditional love.

This insight was the catalyst to a new layer of growth for me. I now understood that negative thinking about myself or others attracted more of that energy. Like attracts like. I was so done with that! Living in such negativity, walking on eggshells—It had to stop. I made the choice.

If you've been drawn to read this book, then it's your time to choose unconditional love, by HONORING YOURSELF using ES Thinking! When there is unconditional love, there is no place for criticism and judgment. The two cannot occupy the same space.

Being in the critical and judgment zone is a habit many people default to automatically. Once we become aware of that default, we have an opportunity to choose love. Now how do we do that? The first step is already done each time we catch ourselves reacting to situations in negative ways whether it be by a particular thought, emotion and/or behavior. Next, validate whatever you are aware of and shift your thoughts to spirit. Is it that easy? Yes, because spirit is always ready to help you. It is only waiting for acknowledgment. That acknowledgement is the beginning of self-love and the gateway to entering the neutral/spirit free zone.

Human psychology is absolutely fascinating to me. Most people say "I love you" to others, but how many times have you said "I love you" to yourself? For many of us, not often, I'll bet. Louise Hay's amazing book, *You Can Heal Your Life*, contains an exercise where you have to face a mirror, look into your eyes, and say, "I love you and accept you exactly as you are." The first time I tried this exercise, I couldn't both meet my eyes and say those words. It actually physically hurt! I kept looking down until I walked away. Eventually, I was able to say it and believe it! Louise Hay stated that the only thing she ever worked on was the concept of *Loving the Self*. She believed that Love is the miracle cure and that Loving Ourselves works miracles in our lives. I am a believer and testament to that. The millions of people Hay has helped are also a testament.

In order to embody self-love, it is important to look inward.

> "Who looks outward, Dreams.
> Who looks inward, Awakens."
>
> ~ Carl Jung

Here are some ways to practice self-love:

☐ Take time each day and set the intention to love yourself. Just setting the intention will bring your attention to it throughout the day.

☐ Journal about what it is like to love yourself:

    ° What does that look like to you?
    ° What thoughts do you hear yourself saying?
    ° How does it feel?
    ° If it is difficult for you to imagine this, then think of someone you love and what you would say to them, and then say those things to yourself.
    ° Make a list of things you can do to show self-love.

My list includes things like:

~ Taking a bath with essential oils and uplifting music
~ Giving myself a facial
~ Taking a walk in nature
~ Journaling what is going on
~ Building a fire and snuggling on the couch without any expectations of doing anything
~ Calling someone just to say hi and share what is going on with each other
~ Having a girls' night out
~ Going to sleep early
~ Meditating

~ Playing with my dog
~ Getting mani/pedis—my personal paradise!

Using the mirror, say loving things to yourself. If you hear yourself thinking negative thoughts, immediately say it again but in the positive. Some examples of my dialogue shifts follow.

~ *How could you lose it like that?* Shifted to:

*Be gentle, Sue. You're only human.*

~ *No wonder you're overweight.* Shifted to:

*Today, I am doing the best I can.*

~ *I should not have said that.* Shifted to:

*I was hurting, but I can apologize.*

I used to say, "fake it till you make it" until I realized that it wasn't real, and I was consistently feeding the negative energy of criticism and judgment. I now live by the motto, "Act as if...." This puts me in the free zone of being positive and living in the energy of unconditional love for myself and others. As I started out acting as if, I then achieved "it."

"Self-care is how you take your power back."

~Lalah Delia

As you connect with loving thoughts for yourself, the easier it gets to feel them. Your thoughts affect your emotions, which affect your behavior. If you are thinking loving thoughts, you have just entered your free zone.

When you decide to be in acceptance and love, whether it be toward yourself or another person or situation, you are in the free zone. When in this zone, you are consciously choosing to think only positive or loving thoughts.

We talked about the importance of awareness and validating our different thoughts, emotions, and behaviors. What drives your thoughts is your perception of a situation or person. This feeds your attitude.

Let's talk about perceptions. We have the critical and judgmental perception zone and the neutral/spirit free zone. The word zone is used to mean any area of your thinking that is separated from one another. You are already moving in and out of these two zones throughout the day; you just weren't as aware of it. Now, you are becoming more aware of your perception in different contexts.

We each have our own model of the world based on our life experiences. For each of us, different situations or people will be more of a trigger than others. This is very individual. That is why it is important to take time to get to know yourself and what your triggers are. What upsets you may not upset another and vice versa.

Who is to say that your way is the right way? Everyone has the right as a human being to view their world in whatever way they want. It is why we each are given freedom of choice.

"Right" and "wrong" are just labels based on judgment. If you remove the words right and wrong and say, "it just is," "it's their preference," you will take the judgment out of it (even if you prefer they do it your way).

You are accepting that, as a fellow human being, they have the right to feel or be however they want. You've probably heard the expression, "Well, I guess we will have to agree to disagree on that." You can, of course, try to convince them of your viewpoint, but at the end of the day, it is their choice whether or not they will agree with you.

Let's look at some examples of the shift that happens with ES Thinking.

**Situation:**

At a party, I remember seeing a male friend being very affectionate with his eleven-year-old daughter. She would sit on his lap and hug him, and they would laugh and have a great time. I was repulsed watching them and thought this was completely inappropriate. I sat in judgment of him and his daughter.

What to do next? Be in the moment. Is the situation having a negative impact on me? Yes, emotionally but not physically. By validating how I felt, I was able to connect with my spirit, release the perception, and refocus on enjoying my experience at the party.

In hindsight, I realized that because I did not have that type of relationship with my father and because of my abuse, I had a distorted view of what that type of relationship should look like. That girl was never abused, and she was blessed with an affectionate father who took time to develop a bond with her.

**Situation:**

My sister and I each have very different parenting styles. I liked schedules and order and had a plan for everything. My sister was the complete opposite. It amazes me that we grew up in the same household. Initially, when she relocated near me, I would lose my mind with the way she was parenting my two nieces. Thankfully, I realized early on that she had a completely different model of the world with regard to parenting. Instead of being critical, I began seeing the positive effects of her style and enjoyed developing a relationship with my nieces. Consequently, my nieces are amazing young women, so how she parented worked for them.

If I did not change my perception, I was on my way to causing a rift between us, which would have denied me the amazing love and relationship I now have with my sister and nieces. Now, I look at my sister in gratitude for all she taught me. I realize that my way works for me, and her way works for her.

Don't miss your own experience by focusing on what is not even yours. Bring your focus inward with gratitude. If you're led by spirit, silently bless everyone's situation; wish everybody well. Now, you have created a more positive energy for yourself that results in a rippling effect for everyone involved. This goes back to "being in it but not of it."

**Situation:**

One person might have been brought up to believe that children are to be seen and not heard. Another person might have been brought up to believe that children should be imaginative and playful and have a say in household matters.

Now let's imagine these two people are out with their kids at a restaurant sitting at tables next to each other. Can you imagine how opposite each table's experiences are? Each parent could easily sit in judgment of the other table. But what's the point? Why even go there? That is just bringing yourself into a place of negativity. Here is where you have a choice. Which scenario would you rather be in? Whatever your answer, it is perfect... perfect for you.

If you see something you don't agree with, instead of criticizing and judging, recognize that your preference is different, based on your model of the world. You'd prefer they were more like you, and guess what? They may be thinking the very same thoughts about you! When you choose free zone thinking, you can decide on the severity of the situation and whether you want to get involved.

Now that you're beginning to understand perception, there is a quick technique to shifting your perception to that neutral/spiritual place. Neutral means impartial. One way to being impartial is to become an observer of your thoughts. We talked about this earlier when you momentarily separated yourself from your thoughts and observed them from a neutral place. I invite you to take some time and practice observing your thoughts from this neutral place connected to spirit. You may be amazed at some of the stuff you think at times!

Every interaction that occurs in our day provides us with information.

**Situation:**

During a period of time when money was scarce, I had twenty dollars left for the week and a few expenses to take care of. I gave it to my fourteen-year-old son to run into a store to get something, and we realized later on that he lost the sixteen dollars change coming out of the store. That was the only cash I had left until payday. I internally freaked and almost went into yelling mode, criticizing him, but I caught myself. I took a breath. Well, maybe a couple of breaths. In that moment, I changed my perception and took in information. I had been actively working on changing my perception of money as a form of energy and to release that attitudes of lack and replace them with the concept of "I have more than enough and then some, and I am grateful." I had the thought that maybe someone who came across this money really needed it.

In that moment, I could have gone into loss and anger regarding all my money issues. But by changing my perception, I actually felt good about that money helping someone else, especially as I knew how grateful I was when someone helped me out financially. The information I gleaned from it was obvious when I told my son, "Moving forward, let's try to be more aware of how we hold onto our money."

It was a powerful moment for me on my journey about perception. I went into a place of acceptance (my heart space) that it happened and reminded myself that I have always been taken care of and will continue to be taken care of. If I stayed in my ego state, I would have ranted about my financial status, and my son would have felt horrible. By going into my spirit, I was able to feel good, and my son hopefully learned a lesson. By the way, by making a few adjustments, I made it fine until payday and had all my family's needs met. Thank you, Higher Power!

**Situation:**

One day, I was talking to a friend's twenty-five-year-old son who was in a bad way. He was sharing how he had been dating two women secretly for over a year and a half. He couldn't live with the lies and secrets anymore and decided to break it off with one and just be with the other. That set off a string of emotions of uncertainty, fear, and anxiety. He couldn't get out of his own way emotionally. His own criticism and judgment of himself were overwhelming him. He was so stuck in his ego state driven by fear, anger, shame, guilt, and anxiety, that he could not move forward. I too had a choice while talking to him. I could have been very judgmental of him and his actions. By moving into my spirit, I could see how, because of a series of human experiences, he found himself in a situation that was hurting himself and others. I focused on his wounds and his desire to change this pattern that had developed in his life. I went to my "impartial" state and looked at him with love. I was then able to help him connect to his heart center free of criticism and judgment and help him shift his perception. Then he was finally able to see a path out of his pain, and his journey to creating the life he wanted began.

We have no idea what other people around us are truly going through in any given moment on any day. We also have no idea what human experiences occurred to them in their lifetime that shaped and molded who they are and their actions. One thing is certain though. Each one of us has an ego, and each one of us has a spirit. We are all one in the same in that regard and have freedom of choice in how we will think, feel, and act. Once we start recognizing these two different states in ourselves and in others, we develop a better understanding of why we act the way we do and why other people act the way they do. This understanding will assist us in going impartial and releasing the criticism and judgment and enter the "free zone." We begin to see our actions and the actions of others as "information."

We get tripped up by our ego by choosing or defaulting to critical and judgmental thinking. When we automatically default to that zone, it is based on our own frame of reference and life experience. We are comfortable with other people who think like us and meet our criteria. We will become friends with those who fit our criteria and stay away from others who don't. That is human nature and the natural flow of life.

The difference with ES Thinking is that you become aware of your thought zones and perceptions throughout your day. Now, you can decide to default into old thought patterns, perceptions, and strategies. When you are in a critical and judgmental zone, you justify your thoughts. This kind of thinking creates emotions that feed your behaviors that do not necessarily serve you in a positive way.

The alternative is choosing Ego Spirit Thinking, that is recognizing old thought patterns (ego) and shifting your intentions and thoughts to spirit. With spirit thinking, there is an acceptance that everything is exactly where we are meant to be. We can acknowledge our old thoughts and behaviors but clearly realize that those programs are outdated. Those outdated programs hurt and can keep us stuck, rather than help. There is a famous saying by Henry Ford, "If you always do what you have always done, you will always get what you've always gotten." Is that insane or what? But so true!

In spirit thinking, we ask ourselves "What do you want? What do you really want?" Now that is the question. By choosing to shift into spirit (unconditional love and acceptance) that puts us into the free zone. When we are in the free zone, we are managing in the moment. This creates a more balanced future that we desire and deserve. Is it that simple? YES! When you decide to do you differently.

Below are more examples of situations whereby moving into my free zone, I was able to create a more positive change:

**Critical and Judgmental Zone:**

I was at work, stressed out, under a time pressure, and kept getting distracted by someone repeatedly interrupting me. I felt myself getting frustrated and starting to lose it. It was in that moment that I heard myself saying things like, "Can't they tell I'm working? I can't get anything done. I should have finished this yesterday before I left."

**Free Zone:**

In that moment, I stopped and took a breath. I was criticizing my coworker and myself. When I realized my thoughts, I closed my eyes and took three deep breaths. I went into my heart space where I felt love and was able to recognize that the other person was stressed as well. I acknowledged I can't change the past, and I called in my higher presence to assist me in the most productive way.

By just taking those few moments, I was able to recognize what I needed and set a boundary with my coworker from a place of peace, not anger. Instead of being a victim of frustration, I took back my power.

I let go of all those critical thoughts of my colleague and myself and was able to focus and allow my higher presence in spirit to step in and assist. The project got done on time.

**Critical and Judgmental Zone:**

I was very frustrated with trying to get my son and myself out of the house on a school morning. I swear no matter how much prep time I gave myself, everything seemed to fall apart in the last five minutes. I would go from a distracted but easy-going mom to a monster, shrieking all kinds of crazy things to my son whether it was his fault or not. Once I saw this pattern emerging, I began to recognize my thoughts. I would say things to myself like, "No matter what, I can't seem to get out on time. One thing always seems to go wrong. My son is taking too long to get ready. Why doesn't he just find everything he needs quicker?" By criticizing and judging my son and me, I was just creating more criticism and judgment and feeding that negative energy.

**Free Zone:**

I started saying positive affirmations about how smoothly our morning will be and how I will get everything done in divine timing and how grateful I am.

Then the miracle happened! I had a smooth morning, and everything was done in divine timing. I was so excited and kept that up as my mantra. Amazingly, it continued.

My son asked me to wake him a little earlier, and I started laying out my work stuff the night before, or I went over what I needed when I was in the shower.

It all happened so organically, and I was thrilled. Now, on that rare occasion when something happens to make us a few minutes late, I take a breath and give it up to my higher power to take care of it. If I am a few minutes late to work, it is not the norm and not a problem. My different thoughts were bringing in a different reality.

**Critical and Judgmental Zone:**

At times, having a teenager is challenging. I think it is a natural reaction at times to want to scream at them, "What? Are you crazy? What were you thinking?"

**Free Zone:**

It is in those moments that I take a breath and interrupt that pattern. By going to my free zone, I can tell myself that teenagers typically don't think. This is how they learn. By going to acceptance and love, I can help him more effectively figure out what happened and what he can do differently next time if he chooses to.

Of course, stuff still comes up at times, but by practicing going to my ES center and taking a breath, I am more easily able to interrupt old patterns and ways of thinking. This has given me more peace and clarity, and I have had to apologize a lot less for my behavior.

Full disclosure. It hasn't lessened his "eye-rolling" one bit or his short attention span when I speak. I just keep re-minding myself that the shift is in me and how I react and how much more I am at peace when dealing with him. That's huge in my world!

I've shared how my sister and I are complete opposites in many ways. Our personalities are different as well. As I mentioned before, I have a tendency to talk a lot. I've shared how I process my world verbally and also how I like order and love to schedule EVERYTHING. If something does not go according to my predetermined schedule, I get stressed. It's one of the many areas I am working on in my self-discovery. Because of these personality traits, I must admit that I can be annoying to be around at times. If you need more confirmation, just ask my brother or my cousin. I real-ized in reflection one day that my sister is one of the few people who does not seem to react to me when I'm in an ex-treme state. I asked her about it one day and how come I don't seem to drive her crazy the way I do other people. She looked at me and said that I used to drive her crazy, but one day she realized that my behaviors were stemming from my own anxiety. They had nothing to do with her, and so she was able to be supportive of me during those times instead of reacting. I was amazed at how by changing her perception, she was able to engage with me during times when others couldn't. I took that lesson forward and remember that whenever I am dealing with someone who is difficult to be around, not to personalize the other person's behavior. That is a signal for me to go into my free zone and connect with my spirit.

> "If you are willing to look at another person's behavior toward you as a reflection of the state of their relationship with themselves rather than a statement about your value as a person, then you will, over a period of time, cease to react at all."

> ~Yogi Bhajan

## Free Zone Exploration:

While answering the following questions, think of a situation where you reacted from your ego state and wish you would have handled things differently. If another person was involved, focus only on your own thoughts, responses, and reactions that occurred during that time.

☐ What were the thoughts I was thinking?

_____

_____

_____

☐ What were the emotions I was feeling?

_____

_____

_____

☐ What behaviors did I exhibit during that experience?

_____

_____

_____

Now, I want you to go to your free zone. Step back and drop into your heart space and connect to your spirit. Look at the same situation again and review the following:

~ Take a breath.
~ Recognize the emotion that is present.
~ Separate from the emotion.
~ Look at the situation impartially, noting what information you're getting from this interaction. See what other information may be going on, besides what you think.
~ Find a positive thought about that situation. ANY positive thought, no matter how hard it may seem.

Next, looking at that situation, answer the following questions:

☐ How would my thoughts be different?

_____

_____

_____

☐ What different emotions am I feeling?

_____

_____

_____

☐ How could my behaviors have changed?

_____

_____

_____

Remember, the purpose of this exercise is not to criticize how you should have done things differently (you would have just left your free zone if you did that). The purpose is to begin seeing how using ES Thinking shifts you into your free zone, that connects to spirit. In your free zone, you will gather the information needed to move through challenging situations with more ease and balance from a place of love.

# 7

## Illusions

"The greatest obstacle to discovery is not
ignorance -it is the illusion of knowledge."

~Daniel J. Boorstin

Illusion means something that is or is likely to be
wrongly perceived or interpreted by the senses.

Wayne Dyer repeatedly stated that the ego is only an illusion. Letting your ego-illusion become your identity can prevent you from knowing your true self. Ego is the false idea
of believing that you are what you have or what you do. He
believed that this is a backward way of assessing and living
life. [1]

---

[1] www.project-meditation.org/10-steps-for-reining-in-your-ego/

Most of our ego-driven thoughts are illusions. While there is a positive intent behind them, those thoughts are based on illusions to keep us "on track." How accurate are those ego-driven thoughts?

Here are some of my prior thoughts and how I processed through the examples:

*I need to protect myself because friends/family/lovers always let me down.*

Although this may be true in some relationships, it is **not** true in all relationships. Because of our expectations of others, based on our model of the world, it is inevitable that some will let us down. By connecting to our spirit, we recognize the illusion of that statement. Once we shift our thoughts, we turn inward and recognize how we can count on ourselves always. By staying in that vibration will bring in more people who will assist us when needed. We also begin to recognize that others are acting in ways because of their own issues and we no longer take it personally.

*No matter what, I can't seem to get out of my house on time.*

Remember back to my story of how my mornings played out with my son? This statement I kept telling myself kept perpetuating that experience. Recognizing that that thought was just an illusion, I was able to change my thoughts, which changed my behaviors, which gave me a totally different result. Now, my mornings are typically easy going, and I am almost always on time. And I'm okay with that!

*It doesn't matter what I do, I never have enough money.*

This thought was so prevalent in my mind for many years. I kept building more and more debt. Once I recognized this thought for the illusion it was, I changed it to, "As money goes out, more than enough comes in which exceeds my needs, and I am grateful." This new thought pattern came straight from my heart and spirit, and before I knew it, options started opening up for me, and I slowly shifted how I viewed and spent money. Over time, as I made changes, positive results began happening, and now I have a budget that I stick to and have stopped accumulating debt. I now live completely within my means.

∞

**Creating your illusion box:**

As I started to connect to my thoughts and recognizing what was truth and what was an illusion, it opened up a whole new way of perceiving my thoughts and experiences. During a call with two of my friends, the concept of an illusion box was introduced to me. We did a guided exercise where I visualized and designed my illusion box. Mine became a rectangular box about six feet long with an ornate jeweled top. There is a button on the top right that, when I press it, automatically opens the door. During the exercise, I placed it next to the door to my garage. I take my garbage out that door! When I recognize a thought or belief I have that is

an illusion, I will (in my mind) take it to my illusion box and
hit the button. I then drop it in and close the door. Then I
visualize it either being transformed into love or being sent
back to the nothingness it came from.

I encourage you to create your own illusion box. Think
of how your box will look and how you will use it. There is
no right or wrong way to do this. It is your own to design as
you see fit.

☐   How big is it?

_____

_____

_____

☐   What shape is it?

_____

_____

_____

☐   Does it have a specific design?

_____

_____

_____

☐   What colors are in it?

_____

_____

_____

☐   How will you open and close the door?

_____

_____

_____

☐   Where will you keep it?

_____

_____

_____

☐   Now think of different thoughts or experiences that you will put in it.

_____

_____

_____

This practice of using my illusion box has helped me to release the illusion and replace it with my truth from a place of unconditional love. I have even used my illusion box to get rid of any energy associated with a nightmare or negative experience.

Full disclosure. I may even have sent a person or two to the illusion box! It's all good. Use it any way that resonates with you. There are no limits!

*Use the next page to draw your own illusion box.*

SUSAN KREBS

**My illusion box:**

# 8.

# Developing a Relationship
# With Our Higher Power/Spirit

"Once you realize there is a Higher Power,
you know you're not alone, that you have a
purpose on the planet. You control your destiny
instead of letting the day lead you where it may.
You seize it, take it, and lead it."

~Queen Latifah

Spirituality is a widespread concept that has many different perspectives. Some people link it with religion, some with
nature, Mother Earth (Gaia) or some may define it as having
a personal relationship with a higher power.  I believe that it

embodies a sense of connection to something bigger than myself, and it has led me on a journey to discover what being human is all about.

My personal definition of spirituality has changed throughout my life. It started out completely linked with religion and has evolved into my belief that God is within each of us in our heart center. Developing and deepening this relationship with my God center or higher power/spirit within me has given me a sense of home that I was looking for.

An ancient Japanese saying states, "There are many paths to the top of the mountain, but the view of the moon from the top is the same." Some may call it intuition, but I believe it is so much more than that. I call it my higher power or spirit. You can call it whatever resonates with you.

Imagine for a moment what it would be like if you were born into a family where your parents were so excited to meet you and were in awe of your magnificence! They felt such incredible love for you every moment of each day. They celebrated every milestone that you experienced as if it happened to them. They saw your struggles and praised you for never giving up. They supported you no matter how many mistakes you made and were a source of unconditional love for every aspect of your personality. Because all their guidance came from that place of unconditional love, they taught you how to navigate life's struggles. They held you when you cried, gave you space when you needed to process, and gave you words of wisdom when you asked. You knew without a shadow of a doubt that you were respected, loved, and never alone. They were always there; all you had to do was reach out to them. They understood your mistakes were not a reflection of who you were and loved you regardless. They never gave up on you or criticized or judged you based on your actions. They taught you how amazing it felt to love and be loved. They taught you how worthy you were of being loved and respected even when you did not agree with their model of what the world should be. They let you find your path and supported you each painful step of the way. They had no expectations of you and let you develop your own sense of self. They did not expect anything in return, for their love was truly unconditional.

Take a few moments and step in and experience this vision. If your mind or ego start passing judgment or comparing it to your own growing up years, just quiet your thoughts, staying in the energy of the vision. What pictures, thoughts, voices, or emotions come up? Reread it as many times as it takes, fully immersing yourself in this scenario.

You may say it is an impossible scenario or even ludicrous. Although it may not have been your own experience growing up, I am here as a witness to let you know that it is being offered to you right now. Your spirit is offering you an opportunity to develop a relationship with your ego and higher power, source energy, and all that God is offering you. This is the relationship that I have with my ego, higher power, and spirit, so I know, firsthand, it is possible. It is not offered to a select few. It is there for everyone to access, and all you have to do is say YES!

You have an opportunity to develop, better understand, or deepen relationships that are important to you right now. This can be done with whomever you want on a spiritual level. All you have to do is say YES. Your higher power will always give you the freedom of choice. It is yours to make. Whether you make it today or later, the offer will always be there. When you say YES, you choose love. Choose love!

Our higher power is that part of us that is connected to

God, source energy, or the universe through spirit. Its purpose is to guide us as humans on our path with greater understanding, peace, and enlightenment. It is what assists us as humans in being in the world but not of it, and it's all good. We have talked about exploring our ego state and spirit state. Our higher power is present when we are in our spirit state and learning how to co-create with ease and grace. Your higher power and spirit are beckoning you to deepen your relationship with self and others at this time.

Your higher power/spirit is not some separate entity that is outside of you, but it is an internal part that is with you 24/7. It is accessible whenever you want to connect with it. You are already connecting with your higher power when you enter your free zone. There is no part of your higher power that criticizes or judges, not even your ego. People connect with their higher power/spirit in a variety of ways. Some may experience a feeling or warmth or chill throughout their body. Some may hear internal dialogues. Some may have visions or see colors, and some may smell a certain scent. There is no right or wrong; your spirit will communicate in ways that are appropriate for you at the right time. We are connecting to our higher power in those moments that spontaneously happen to us when we are in a place of love, beauty, and acceptance.

Now that you are aware of connecting and learning how to develop your relationship with your higher power, you will realize that you are never truly alone.

Loneliness, anxiety, and fear are so prevalent in our human existence. They are some of the drivers that hold us in a criticism and judgment zone. That's when we are pushed toward external attachments and material possessions to make us feel better.

When we are in the free zone, there is an internal connection to our spirit that connects to our higher power. That's when our spirit can fulfill our needs and then some with self-love.

In an article written by Gretchen Rubin, she states in order to be happy, we need intimate bonds, we need to be able to confide, we need to feel that we belong, and we need to be able to get and give support. Having strong relationships is key — perhaps the key — to a happy life. When we are disconnected from others in some way, it causes anxiety, fear, and loneliness. There are many different reasons for this disconnection. You could have moved into a new place or job situation, or you may feel as if you are different than others and don't fit in. You may be single and wishing for a life partner. You may be having difficulty connecting with those around you due to your own actions or those actions of others, or you might be missing that closeness you had with someone in your past. [2]

By connecting with your higher power in love, you naturally extend that connection out to others and attract that connection vibrating with love back to you. It all begins within you first.

By taking the time to be alone, free from distraction, you are beginning this journey of discovery. There are no two ways about it. In order to connect to your higher power, you have to take time to be alone with your thoughts and all that comes along with it. You are starting to deepen your relationship with that part of yourself that is bigger than your

---

[2] https://www.psychologytoday.com/us/blog/the-happiness-project/201702/7-types-loneliness-and-why-it-matters

limited human experience. I always tell my son that knowledge is power. By accessing the information we receive by spending time alone, we are taking our power back and co-creating with our spirit. The life we want more than anything all starts with creating time and taking moments to connect with that part of us that is all-knowing. You are worth it! I have a saying in my kitchen: "It will cost you nothing to believe and everything not to." Just try it. Be alone. Connect to your higher power and spirit. Watch the beauty unfold as you process through the layers of ES Thinking.

It is important to differentiate that being alone does not mean the same as being lonely. A friend once told me he was terrified of being alone. But after talking about it, he was really terrified of being lonely, which is the *feeling* of being alone. We as a society have, over time, linked the two concepts as one in the same. Rubin gives a beautiful description of the difference: loneliness feels draining, distracting, and upsetting whereas desired solitude feels peaceful, creative, and restorative. [3]

When we take quiet time alone, we become more centered and connected. There's a sense of wholeness and peace because we are creating and building a relationship between our ego and spirit. This ES relationship is where we improve our ability to reflect and move forward on our path with understanding and acceptance, that place of enlightenment. All this while having a human experience with love that ripples out into the world.

We as humans are trained to avoid uncomfortable feelings of pain, loss, fear, guilt, anger, and resentment. When we

[3] https://www.psychologytoday.com/us/blog/the-happiness-project/201702/7-types-loneliness-and-why-it-matters

are lonely and perceive ourselves as being alone, we think that we must avoid that at all costs. So, we create behaviors that help us deal with those negative emotions. When these behaviors are driven by our ego, they typically provide relief in the moment, but in the bigger scheme of our lives, they are not serving us in the best way.

Negative emotions typically manifest themselves in extremes:

~ Isolating ourselves or keeping super busy in order to avoid.
~ Over thinking a situation to death and creating chaos and confusion in our thoughts.
~ Distracting ourselves with mindless actions like binge watching TV, being on social media, sleeping, eating, smoking, taking drugs, or overspending.

How many of the above behaviors can you identify with? Are you aware when negative emotions occur? Have some of those behaviors become a habit that you justify, despite the consequences? The above are examples of how your thoughts trigger emotions that, in turn, drive your behavior.

It is important to remember that those thoughts and behaviors have a positive intent. The intent is to stop and manage the pain or fear in some way. Once you identify those thought patterns and behaviors, you're empowered to do emotions differently—or not—based on your thoughts. You have a choice.

When we choose to be in our heart center and connected to our higher power, we create an intimate bond with our spirit. No matter what happens in our daily life, we have the keys to access our higher power that is always there for us.

We are never alone. Once we become receptive and connect to our heart center, the magic happens. We are guided and have tools that help us navigate through struggles and challenges that are all part of our human journey. This is what we mean when we say we are spiritual beings having a human experience.

I first started consciously connecting to my higher power about fifteen years before writing this book. I say consciously, because although I always had this higher power within me, I did not recognize it and was always looking outward at some external source to guide me. What helped to shift my awareness to my higher power was trying a yoga class and hearing about meditation and its positive results. I began researching it and found that most people were either really into it or not at all. There was not much of an in-between stage there. My experience was also that I became cautious of who I spoke to about it because many would make fun of the concepts. Times have really changed, and I am so excited for these shifts.

"5 Ways to Deepen Your Connection to the Divine," an article by Christine Hassler, speaks of a spiritual teacher who beautifully defined this connection to our higher power. His name is Arkan, and he said, "To me, what spirituality is really about is one's capacity to be guided." [4] This resonated so strongly with me. Developing our relationship with our higher power is, in essence, looking at our capacity to be guided.

You don't have to go to church, meditate, pray, fast, juice, eat organically, go to yoga, chant, or live in a commune

---

[4] https://www.mindbodygreen.com/0-21233/5-ways-to-deepen-your-connection-to-the-divine.html

to connect with your higher power. Those are just external factors that may or may not help facilitate your connection with the guidance your higher power is giving you. Those behaviors are individual and are made of your own free will and choice. If it works for you, go for it! You may even find over time that one or more of those practices do help!

What is important is to be open to explore what helps you connect to that guidance of spirit. Many times, as we explore, we become aware of what gets in the way or may just be illusions. It's all about learning how to do life differently. Or not!

In order for you to deepen your relationship with your higher power, consider doing the following:

Let go of your expectations and release any attachments to the way you think things should be. This can be difficult for some because when we think we know the way things should be, we feel more in control. Unfortunately, this sense of control is an illusion. The only thing we have control over is our thoughts and reactions to what life offers us on a daily basis. Anything else we tell ourselves is a lie based on our need to feel safe.

"Sometimes you have to let go of the picture
of what you thought it looked like and learn to find
joy in the story you are actually living."

~tinybuddha.com

When I started consistently connecting to my higher power, I began to realize that I was always focused on the future. I was married at that time, with an infant son and stepchildren, working fulltime, and managing my spouse's extended family's needs as well as my own extended family's needs. I was trying to pay bills and keep up with cleaning, cooking, and laundry. Spend time alone? I thought. "Yeah right! That's a pipe dream!" If I did get time alone, I either fell asleep or tried to play catch up on my multitude of responsibilities. It was always about what was next because the list was ENDLESS! Looking back, I also realize that in the beginning when I stopped and took those moments to be alone, my thoughts scared the hell out of me. I had some really scary, angry, unhappy thoughts. It was easier to avoid that and focus on the list of all external things that needed to be done to avoid what was bubbling under the surface. Perhaps you can relate.

By focusing on the future, I could just push down what my negative thoughts were telling me about the present I wanted to avoid. I had trained myself to believe that I was living "the dream" and always focused on what was next or telling myself, "If I only do this, or if this happens, I will be happier." In retrospect, what I was really doing was letting my ego be the driver. I was giving my power to external sources to determine what my life should look like. No wonder I was so unhappy. Many people define happiness as a feeling of wellbeing and contentment. I was never satisfied and never felt that contentment. I had been doing this my whole life. I adopted roles based on external factors to determine how I could be "happy." The consequence was that I was missing how I could find joy and peace in the present day by taking my power back and being in the moment.

Hindsight is such a beautiful thing. OK, that was written with a total sarcastic edge! Seriously though, as I reflect on my journey in connecting with my higher power, I realize that my spirit is my own personal cheerleader. My spirit is loving me unconditionally and giving me the safe space to feel what I need to feel, guiding me to what is true and what is an illusion, and supporting me as I continue to discover who the real me is. Now, I am more present in the moment, experiencing joy in what is happening right now. In the present, I can release fears of the future, knowing that I am loved and always taken care of. This is co-creating with spirit in the "NOW" moment. I finally learned how to love myself.

"Turn your wounds into wisdom."

~Oprah Winfrey

Emotions are a part of life. They drive us. Are you aware of when and why emotions occur? We all experience emotions from time to time. They are associated with negative and positive thoughts that trigger feelings and behavioral responses. How we think has an impact on how we feel. One of the first emotions we learn instinctively is fear. When we are born, we are suddenly exposed to pain, and we cry.

Did you know love is a choice as well as a feeling? Feelings come and go, but choosing love, unconditional love, is steady. Love is an act; it is deliberate. It's committing to your spirit/higher self-consciously deciding what's best to do—or not to do.

We default to an emotional reality that's based on past experiences and environment at the time. We feel them, but we are given the choice as a humans on how we deal with them. We can push them away, avoid them, ignore them, or we can embrace them and validate them, release them, heal them, and shift them at any given moment. It is all about our perception and our focus. I can say from my own experience that pushing them away and avoiding them is EXHAUST-ING. The energy we spend in doing this creates a vortex of negativity, and all it ends up doing is forcing us to make choices that are not in our highest good and cause more issues in the long run.

When I reflect back on my first marriage, I felt as if I was completely unworthy, and that it was my role to provide for and take care of my husband. I pushed away and ignored my feelings of resentment, anger, and unworthiness, and because of my sense of responsibility, kept on thinking that if I just did more, I would feel happy. By not addressing how I was feeling, I evolved into this angry person who did not like the man I married and was so tired of being taken advantage of. I turned to external sources to cope and started smoking again and using food to self soothe. I learned important lessons from that relationship but ended up hurting my ex-husband whom I cared about, and myself more in the process. I never let myself process the feelings of anger, hurt, resentment, and grief and jumped right into a relationship with a man who would eventually become my second husband. On the outside, my second husband appeared to be the polar opposite of my first husband, and I thought I had finally found the one who would make me happy. Remember I was still thinking that external factors would bring me the happiness I sought. I was looking for my happiness outside of myself. I was older and knew more about myself, and so for a while, I was happier. Again, as Henry Ford said, "If you always do what you've always done, you'll always get what you've always gotten." Well, here I was in a relationship again where I avoided fear and anger and looked to external factors to make me feel happy. I avoided conflict as much as possible and because of my sense of responsibility, put myself and my needs last because I thought if I did more, I would feel happier. When I didn't, I continued to turn to external factors to help cope. I kept on smoking, kept on using food to self soothe. Ten years later, I was back to being that angry person who felt like I was always being taken advantage of. The only difference was now I had stepsons, as well as my son to consider. How would all the painful implications of divorce affect them?

Although the external details of my life with both husbands were very different, the themes and wounds that I re-enacted and suffered from were eerily similar. Again, I found myself hurting, my second husband hurting, and now my stepchildren and son were hurting.

Thankfully, I had started connecting more consistently with my spirit and through love and guidance, I was able to realize I needed to do something different if I wanted a different result. It was time to be alone and figure this whole thing out. My first step was connecting with my emotions, especially the ugly, scary ones. Because of my spirit connection, I knew I was not alone and would be guided through this process. It was time to turn my wounds into wisdom and start moving forward.

"Faith and fear both demand that you believe in
something that you cannot see. You choose."

~Bob Proctor

When you decide to choose faith and connect with your higher power and spirit, you also choose unconditional love. You begin making changes in your life with the help of your inner guidance from a place of self-love. It will feel scary at times but with faith and love, it all works out for your highest good.

When your ego is the driver of your thoughts, you experience fear. When your higher power and spirit is the driver of your thoughts, you experience faith.

**What is fear?**

Mary Demetria Davis always reminded me that fear is:

**F: False**
**E: Evidence**
**A: Appearing**
**R: Real**

False evidence appearing real. When we are stuck in fear or feel anxiety, we are either focusing on the past or worrying about the future. One or the other...that is the bottom line. Think about it… bring to mind a situation that evokes fear and ask yourself is this wrapped up in the details of my past or is a worry about something in the future? We may be afraid something is going to happen in the future because of our past beliefs. Fear can also be invoked because some elements in our life feel out of our control.

Here are a few examples of how my ego was using fear to drive my behavior:

~ *What if my son gets hurt playing football?*
~ *How am I going to pay this month's bills?*
~ *What if this person I love dies?*

Take each of those statements and look at them as false evidence appearing real. They "appear real" because it could totally happen. I invite you to allow your faith to be stronger than your fear. Your faith comes from your spirit that loves you and takes care of you. Release your fears and anxiety and shift your focus by bringing the situation into the "now" moment. Look at the situation from a perspective of gathering information in the free zone. Remain open, and your spirit will provide guidance as to what to do next.

In the moment, ask yourself, is it happening right now? Is my son hurt right now? Do I have to pay those bills today? Shifting your attention into this moment is the first part of accessing your faith. The next is about what information and guidance you're receiving from spirit.

*What if my son gets hurt playing football?*

I used to be petrified that my son was going to be hurt while playing football. I cringed and worried, and sure enough, he got hurt repeatedly, including once being taken off the field in an ambulance. Talk about thoughts creating our reality! I was never so relieved when he stopped playing. A couple of years later, after learning how to shift my fear to faith, he started playing lacrosse. They actually beat the crap out of each other with sticks in that game! I remembered how I used to be during the football games and decided to call on my faith. Instead of worry or fear, I started saying a quick prayer before each game and surrounding him in a bubble of God's light, love, and protection. Instead of fear, I sent him the energy of love, light, and protection. I knew that if he was hurt, we would get through it, no matter what. With that knowledge, I began really getting into the game and found myself among the other parents screaming, "CHECK HIM, CHECK HIM!!" (Which means to hit the other player with your stick!), I had no fear and was able to get into the excitement of the game. It became a great experience for both my son and me. I have carried this forward to include all sports he participates in. So far, so good. Regardless though, we will get through whatever comes our way because God's got our back.

### How am I going to pay this month's bills?

I have had my share of financial issues and fears. I can remember many times feeling gripped with fear, paralyzed with worry and anxiety, and frozen. The only way I knew how to cope was to smoke, drink, eat, binge watch TV, or spend more on credit cards. (I know it does not make sense, but I was unaware of my patterns at the time.) I could not see a way out. I would allow my fears to feed avoidance behaviors. By starting out and moving into the now moment, I realized I was bringing up all my financial worries for the next six months. I began connecting with how I was feeling and what I was thinking. I decided to be in the moment, to "Be here now." Not past or future, just now.

Once I brought my focus into the present, I focused only on what needed to be paid currently. I started saying the mantra, "As money goes out, more than enough comes in that exceeds my needs, and I am grateful." By shifting my focus from fear to faith, I started talking to my spirit, and ideas started coming to me. I would get an email out of the blue about finances, or I would overhear someone talking about a financial avenue I never thought to explore.

By connecting to my higher power, I realized I wasn't alone as a single mom. I kept chunking it down to the moment and what I needed to take care of today. Over time, I realized that through my faith, God had a plan for me to get out of debt. I started receiving information about my beliefs about money, which connected me to my thoughts and emotions that drove my behaviors. I took back my power by obtaining information. Knowledge is power! By acknowledging my feeling and changing my thoughts, I changed my behaviors. Don't get me wrong. There has been an ebb and flow to my financial path. When the ebb occurred, I recognized I would drop back into fear and let my ego drive again. By releasing fear thinking, I was able to move into faith thinking, letting my spirit drive. When I was in the moment connected to spirit, I received all kinds of information that helped me to get back on my action plan. Now, I am living within my means without any external credit card debt for the first time in my entire life. I am also managing unexpected expenses more resourcefully.

### *What if this person I love dies?*

I'll never forget the day my dad told me he was diagnosed with esophageal cancer. The memory is forever imprinted in my mind. I told you earlier that he was a violent alcoholic during my growing up years. We had a tumultuous relationship throughout my school years. When I graduated from high school, he went into a rehab program for the final time and, for the rest of his life, never drank again. Throughout my college years and into adulthood, we had a decent relationship that consisted of weekly to biweekly phone calls and periodic visits because I moved 2 ½ hours away from him. There was a layer of superficiality to our relationship, but underneath it all, we both loved each other very much.

Up to that point of his diagnosis, I played the role well of a dutiful daughter, not rocking the boat. When I found out, I was devastated but I immediately went into the role of cheerleader and Miss Positivity. He was going to fight this and win. End of story. Well, that was not the end of the story. He lived one-month shy of two years from the date of his diagnosis. While I wouldn't want anyone to ever be diagnosed with cancer, the reality of his condition forced me to realize how precious life is and what is truly important in a relationship. His diagnosis put a spotlight on the dynamics of our relationship and made me want to go deeper with him.

Over the next two years, we were able to reach an understanding of what had happened all those years growing up and forgive each other for whatever human failings we had. In essence, we started fresh and got to enjoy each other's company on a deeper level fully grounded in the now moment, knowing that there was a higher power that would take care of all the details beyond the now. Of course, there were some rough points in this journey. The more I recognized when my ego was driving my thoughts and behaviors, the easier it became to let my spirit and higher power take over the wheel. My higher power also helped me to recognize when my dad's ego was his driver, and I did not take things so personally. This enabled me to understand how to experience unconditional love for my dad. As soon as I connected to my spirit, the road would smooth out again.

94

At some point, we will all die. By grounding ourselves in the now moment with faith and love, we will manage whatever difficulties come our way. Although I wish my dad did not have to suffer, I will always cherish those two years.

**Simple ways to foster our connection to our Higher Power/Spirit:**

☐ Take time to sit quietly and comfortably. Any time, any place is good for this. Next time you have a few minutes, instead of looking at texts, emails, or social media, just sit quietly in the space you are in. If it is difficult to go inward, look around. If you find yourself criticizing something, interrupt that pattern and look for a beautiful sight or anything that makes you smile. The energy of your higher power/spirit is there in that beauty.

☐ Throughout the day, ask your higher power questions of how to handle a situation or just check in and see what type of response you get. Remain curious. Remember to let go of any expectations of what that might look like. Be open minded.

☐ Tune into what signs and symbols you receive.

~ It could be a picture comes to mind.
~ You might hear a voice in your head or your own voice talking.
~ All of a sudden, a certain song might come on the radio that is perfectly in line with what you were looking for.

~ You could notice a repeating number showing up or see an animal that is unusual, and you might feel the desire to look up the symbolism of what it means.

~ A book or paper might fall off your table, and you might be drawn to a certain page.

~ Out of the blue, you may run into someone or get a call, and that person you encounter might help you figure out how to handle a situation.

Your higher power/spirit is always guiding you to move toward a higher and deeper version of who you are. Its purpose is to guide you in the direction of what is in your highest good even if you do not like your current circumstances. By letting your higher power lead, you are always guided to the best version of who you are.

If you're uncertain if a message is from your higher power, check in with how you feel. Any messages you receive from your higher power will use unconditional love, acceptance, beauty, and excitement to deliver it to you. If you feel any negative emotion, your ego just stepped in to intercept the message.

☐ Begin by taking a couple of minutes when you first wake up or right before bed to tune into your heart center and let go of any worries or negative thoughts that may creep up. Imagine yourself breathing in love and exhaling out any negative thoughts or emotions. Just focus on breathing. Then, create an image of your higher power or listen in to see what your higher power has to share with you in the energy of love. Connect with whatever feelings your higher power wants to share with you. End with thanking your higher power for anything that comes to mind.

☐ Meditation is also a sure-fire way to connect with your higher power. When I started my practice fifteen years ago, I could not sit for more than two minutes without feeling like I was crawling out of my skin. I read a couple of books on how to focus on my breathing, let my thoughts come in, place a bubble around them and watch them float away, but those books did not really help. I would start to get distracted by the bubbles! If I was able to stay in a relaxed state, I typically fell asleep. Full disclosure: I still fall asleep at times. I decided to try guided meditations. I started with Doreen Virtue's chakra-clearing meditation and did that for almost a year. They were twenty-minutes long, and I started off doing it once or twice a week and worked myself up to every morning and/or night. Now, you can Google meditation and have a plethora of options. My suggestion would be to choose one that is by a known person in the field or someone you trust until you start to build your own resources. Over time, I started going to meditation classes and began seeing the positive shifts that occurred. I was hooked! Now, I can meditate pretty much anytime, anywhere and intuitively get everything I need from it. It's another game changer for me! If you're feeling guided to try it, be gentle with yourself and trust that you will be guided to whatever way works for you. It's a process. Enjoy each step.

- ☐ Praying is a beautiful way to connect with your higher power if this resonates with you. While praying, be cognizant of how much talking you are doing and how much listening is going on. It is in the listening that the messages come through, and you can access that guidance that is being given to you.

- ☐ Help someone out. Whenever you help others, you focus on something other than yourself. When you help other people, in that moment, you are cultivating a direct line to understanding a higher power. In that moment when you feel the beautiful energy of gratitude and caring from another, you realize you are a part of something much greater.[5]

The more you take time to develop your relationship with your spirit, the deeper it will become. It's like having the best parts of your closest friend with you at all times without all the annoying traits! Recognizing each state and observing how we are moving back and forth between our ego and spirit in different situations is what ES Thinking is all about. It is learning about and co-creating with your higher power to achieve a better, more fulfilled life with ease and grace.

---

[5]https://sobernation.com/finding-a-higher-power-a-personal-account-of-god-and-recovery/

# 9

## Gratitude

"Gratitude unlocks the fullness of life.
It turns what we have into enough, and more.
It turns denial into acceptance, chaos to order,
confusion to clarity. It can turn a meal into a feast,
a house into a home, a stranger into a friend. Gratitude
makes sense of our past, brings peace for today,
and creates a vision for tomorrow."

~Melody Beattie

Gratitude is another way to use ES Thinking to create positive change in your life. Gratitude is the quality of being thankful; it is also defined as the readiness to show appreciation for and to return kindness. We have talked about how our thoughts create emotions and our emotions drive our behaviors. By engaging in thoughts of gratitude, we see things with more light that trigger positive emotions. We begin behaving in more resourceful, positive ways as a result. Our half-empty glass becomes half-full, and that is the shift.

Multiple studies have explored the positive impacts that gratitude has on us as human beings. It can help us release toxic emotions, and it is considered a powerful tool for relating to others. People who easily come from a place of gratitude tend to be more agreeable and open minded. Being thankful can give us the resolve we need to make better choices in our lives and for the ones we love in the most amazing ways.

Have you heard of the Law of Attraction? The Law of Attraction (very basic definition) is the belief that by focusing on positive or negative thoughts, people can bring positive or negative experiences into their lives. Remember my stories about my son getting hurt during football or how crazy our mornings were? All I can say is that when I changed my thoughts and emotions about each situation, I brought about change, and I was so thankful. I just kept saying "thank you" whenever I thought about it. It deepened the experience by having gratitude for the outcome.

Practicing gratitude toward my higher power and spirit has totally reduced the levels of stress in my life. I started out with just adding the catchphrase on the end of my prayers… "And I am grateful." It helped me to get into the habit of expressing gratitude. I noticed that when I added gratitude in my prayers that my positive energy flow deepened. When I surround my son in a bubble of God's light, love, and protection, I feel good. Then when I say, "thank you," and "I am so grateful," it actually magnifies that good feeling I am experiencing.

Expressing gratitude during good times is easier and is a great way to start getting into the habit of shifting into and recognizing the energy of gratitude. It can be more difficult during emotionally challenging moments. Also challenging is when you and another person are involved in a negatively charged interaction. Sometimes, my gratitude statement is, "I am grateful that meeting is over." Or when I have been desperate, my statement was, "I am so grateful that I am alive and breathing right now!"

Seeing how much better I felt when I was in a place of gratitude, I started challenging myself to find something to be grateful for in every situation:

- When the lesson I taught bombed, and the session was a disaster, my gratitude statement was, "I am so grateful to have the knowledge never to do that again!"
- When an unexpected bill came up, and I had to take money from my Christmas club to pay it, my gratitude statement was, "Thank you, God, that I had the funds to pay this bill. I am grateful that you will provide the funds to buy presents when the time comes." I was able to get all that I needed that holiday season.
- When I was so sick and had to take a week off work to heal, and I could get nothing else done, my gratitude statement was, "I am grateful to have a job that pays me for time off when I am sick."
- When my dad died, I was so grateful for the time we had together in the end, and it helped ease my grief.
- When my son made some choices that caused a tremendous amount of stress in our home, I was so grateful that the lesson he learned had a minimal amount of collateral damage.

Gratitude shifts us out of the negative and into a more positive energy flow, which allows us to avoid getting stuck and to move forward from a place of love.

> "You can't have a bad attitude when you're in Gratitude. The two do not co-exist. It's a choice."

> -~Mary Demetria Davis

∞

## Gratitude Exploration:

☐ Think of three situations that occurred during your day today.

_____

_____

_____


☐ Looking at one event at a time, think about what emotions you were experiencing during that event.

_____

_____

_____

☐ Say one thing you're grateful for because of that happening. You can start with, "Thank you for…" or "I am grateful for…."

_____

_____

_____

☐ Now go through the situation again and add in your gratitude statement. Notice the emotions you're feeling when experiencing gratitude. Describe what is happening in your mind and body.

_____

_____

_____

The more you move into the feeling of gratitude, the more gratitude you feel. I swear, I am living proof. When my son was thirteen, he and I were talking in the car one day. I was attempting to impart "great words of wisdom" to him. In all his beautiful honesty (aka: disgusted teenager tone paired with the appropriate eye rolling), he said, "Mom, I just can't be all positive like you every day!" While I wished he was getting my message, I was so excited because I wasn't even aware of how much I was incorporating gratitude into my daily practice until he reflected it back to me! As a side note, recently I was talking to Kyle about something I was upset with him about, and at one point, he turned to me and started his response with, "Mom, let's look at the positive side…." I was completely taken aback. Then, as I reflected how right he was, I have to admit that I was internally chuckling at how he must be getting it on some level. Of course, I did not let him know that. I was just so grateful! Full disclosure. Even though he was totally using my words to attempt to get out of trouble, I took solace in the fact that a seed is planted somewhere in that brain of his.

I challenge you to try it. Leave yourself notes in your car or on your bathroom mirror and when you see one of those notes, think of one, two, or three things you are grateful for. Don't just fake it. Make it something real, even if it something like, "I am grateful for toilets and running water." Let the magic of this shift be a part of who you are and watch how the universe gives you more things to be grateful for.

# 10

## Releasing and Healing the Past

"In the process of letting go, you will lose many
things from the past, but you will find yourself."

~Deepak Chopra

So far, we have discussed how to increase our awareness
of when we are in our ego and spirit state and have explored
the positive intent behind both. We have practiced how to
bring ourselves into the Now moment and delved into our
critical/judgment zones and free zones. We are now developing and deepening our relationship with spirit with gratitude. These concepts and practices are what I call the foundation when building our house on an ES Center. Now, it is

time to examine what old paradigms you need to let go of in order to continue this journey.

We discussed earlier the importance of recognizing what our thoughts are, connecting to the emotions that are triggered so we can see how these emotions drive our behaviors. You have read at different points how we need to change our perception of pain and hardship. As we expand our awareness, we begin recognizing them as opportunities for growth.

You have also read how important it is to identify the emotions, validate them, and release them. Well, what does that mean exactly? How do we validate and release emotions? For me, that was the most difficult part. It's easier said than done at first, but with practice, it became a big-time game changer.

In order to fully understand "releasing emotions," I need to digress into Quantum Physics for a moment. Science has always put me to sleep, so trust me when I say this will be brief!

### Everything is energy!

**LearningMind.com** gives the following definition:

> "Quantum Physics proves that solid matter does not exist in the universe. Atoms are not solid, in fact, they have three different subatomic particles inside them: protons, neutrons, and electrons. The protons and neutrons are packed together into the center of the atom, while the electrons whizz around the outside. The electrons move so quickly that we never know exactly where they are from one moment to the next. In reality, the atoms that form objects and

substances that we call solid are actually made up of 99.99999% space."[6]

Everything is made of atoms, which are energy—this shows us that everything is made up of energy. The energy that makes you is the same energy that composes trees, rocks, the chair you are sitting on, and the phone, computer, or tablet you may be using to read this. It's all made of the same stuff – energy."

We are all energy, and each interaction we have throughout the day is an exchange of energy. Whether you are talking with a friend or hugging a tree, you are exchanging energy. Lorie Ladd in her YouTube video, "Releasing the Past and Subtle Bodies" explains that humans take in information from energy and processes it through different "bodies" or aspects of ourselves.

While I had heard it all before in different ways, her explanation clarified the process for me. I related so strongly to what happens when we have an experience and how to process through it. Below is my interpretation.

When we are born, we immediately begin having experiences that start to shape who we become.

All day long we are having energy exchanges, day after day. I can't even imagine at forty-nine years old, what the total number of exchanges I have had in this lifetime. My exchanges have ranged from easy to process through to complete dissociation and everywhere between! Given my history, there have been many experiences I did not process through to completion.

---

[6]www.learning-mind.com/everything-is-energy/

Not fully processing the sexual abuse of my childhood resulted in a long string of unhealthy relationships with men and two divorces.

I invite you to shift your perception of how you experience your day in terms of the different types of energy exchanges you have.

Each experience has to filter through three aspects of yourself in order to be fully processed. The denser and more traumatic the experience, the slower the process. They are:

1. Physical body (human body)
2. Emotional body (your emotions)
3. Mental body (your thoughts)

For us to fully process an experience, we have to be aware of our feelings in the present, totally in the "NOW" moment.

Lorie Ladd gives the example of a child who gets bitten by a dog. In **her physical body**, she feels the pain of the bite and may replay seeing the dog's teeth on her. **Her emotional body** may be feeling scared, angry, fearful, or anxious. **Her mental body** may be thinking, "Dogs are scary, they bite people, they are unfriendly, dogs are not safe."

If the **child didn't process** the energy of that experience through her three bodies to completion, the trauma would remain in one or more of the bodies. Fast forward ten years, and this teenager still has an intense fear of dogs that is triggered whenever she sees one. She may have been bitten by a second or third dog.

If the **child processed** through the energy of the experience to completion, and we fast forward ten years, she may have been cautious around unfamiliar dogs but would have been able to manage her emotions. She might have even had dogs of her own and have many loving memories associated with them.

## WHEN do you know you have processed an experience to its completion?

Looking back at the themes that have played out in my relationships with men, have I felt it and processed it through to completion? Yes, I can say I have. How do I know? I look back on all my relationships with men and instead of feeling pain, shame, fear, abandoned, angry, and unworthy, I feel love. Most important, love for myself as well as love for them as human beings being a part of my growth. I also feel this sense of freedom unlike I have felt before with respect and unconditional love for myself. I am so grateful for this.

Full disclosure. What I have described above was a bit of a process. It did not happen overnight. It was difficult at times to sit in the feelings. I would dissociate at times and fall into the old habit of criticizing myself or others.

Understanding the process helped me to get back on track, allowing and releasing the gamut of emotions I had been holding onto for so long. It was like unpeeling layers of an onion, a complete healing process.

Let's be realistic here. While we are on this journey, most of us still must work, take care of family and all the other responsibilities and challenges that come with life. It's easier said than done to take the time to process or be gentle with ourselves. Just remember, **you deserve it! ANY** time you take to move through the process is a step forward toward feeling it to completion.

Think of something that happened to you recently that was upsetting at the time but no longer upsets you.

- ☐ Did you vent to a friend and work through it?
- ☐ Did you journal about it?
- ☐ Did you go for a walk or run?
- ☐ Did you work out or clean your house like an obsessed mad person as you were going over the experience in your mind?
- ☐ Did you talk it out with the person?

Whatever you did, you processed it to completion and gained some insight since you no longer have a reaction about it.   When you no longer have a physical, emotional, or mental reaction to the experience, it is done.   It's all good, and each experience was an opportunity to grow and learn from love and acceptance of self.

**Let's talk about HOW to process through the energy of an experience and what that looks like, sounds like, and feels like.**

There are two components to the "HOW."   One is the thought process that we each use to explore how we do us. The other is the actions we take or tools we use to accelerate our moving through an experience to completion.

**Sit in and FEEL all aspects of the experience, feeling it to completion.**

- ☐ Bring yourself into the Now moment and explore your thoughts.

- ☐ Go to that neutral/impartial place and observe your thoughts.
- ☐ What is truth, and what is an illusion?
- ☐ What belief system do you have that is encouraging these thoughts?
- ☐ What emotions are you feeling?
- ☐ Is there criticism or judgment about yourself or others?
- ☐ Shift into spirit thinking (unconditional love and acceptance), which shifts you into the free zone.

When you are in the free zone, you will be more aware and managing in the moment. Once in the free zone, you have laid the groundwork to release and heal.

There is no right or wrong feeling, no right or wrong thought, no right or wrong way to do this. It is your unique process. Honor yourself as you learn how you do you.

Depending on the experience, it could take you two minutes, two hours, two days, two months, or longer. Again, there is no right or wrong timeframe. It is all very individual, a **subjective experience.** You and a friend could both break up with a boyfriend at the same time, and she may have processed it in two weeks, while you may have taken three months. People process differently. That's it!

A typical behavior we default to when going through a difficult experience is dissociation. The more difficult the experience, the easier it is to disassociate. Who wants to stay in their body feeling crappy, connected to their yucky thoughts? Not I! I was queen of dissociation. I had it down to a science. I would keep myself busy, sleeping, smoking, eating, drinking, or spending money to avoid my thoughts and feelings. My ego was in the driver's seat with the intent to help me avoid the pain so I could keep managing my life. The dissociation helped me deal/manage in the moment, but it stopped me from processing traumatic events to completion.

I held onto the trauma on some level within my body. I continued to have more traumatic events, and they just piled up one on top of the other. The problem was, I kept on repeating negative patterns and causing more pain to dissociate from. Certain emotions like fear, anger, lack of trust, sadness, etc. triggered my need to dissociate.

In some ways, I was a hamster spinning my wheels and not getting far. Not processing the experiences completely stopped me from experiencing freedom and liberation from my past.

Moving forward, the beautiful news is that we don't have to revisit every traumatic event that we ever experienced in our lives to release and heal. It is easy to get caught up in the "story" of our experience and start to relive it as if we are in it again. Frankly, that scared me, and I would have said, "No thank you. I'll stay dysfunctional!"

What we can do is become aware of the different themes that trigger us and are being played out in our lives. Remember the stories of my two divorces? Totally opposite men, but the same themes were being played out. When I took time to be alone, I realized that those same themes were played out in most of my relationships going back to high school. By taking the time to be in the "Now" moment, I was able to *feel* my feelings. I connected with my thoughts. I began recognizing when I was being critical of myself and moved into my free zone. Some of my thoughts were total illusions based on fear, not fact. Some of my thoughts were based on belief systems that were not true and didn't support me in positive ways. I started loving and honoring myself wherever I was. I felt the guidance of my spirit bringing people into my life to help me gain more clarity. I began treating myself the way I wanted a partner to treat me—with kindness and respect.

I still have contact with my son's father because we co-parent together. Our relationship is not Utopia, and at times, we may get annoyed or frustrated with each other, but I am no longer reactive based on the past, and we have a working relationship focusing on each other's strengths (to the best of our abilities; we are human, after all!).

You have been reading all about this process and the steps involved in processing through, and while the steps are universal, the "how" piece is very individual. Below is a collection of activities that will help you process through the energy of an experience when moving through the steps discussed above.

Ask yourself the following questions:

☐ How do I allow an experience to filter through?
☐ How do I process an experience energetically and move through my physical, emotional, and mental body?

In order to start this process, it is important to take time to relax. Schedule quiet time for yourself, at least five to twenty minutes a day. For some, this will be easier to do than others. If it is harder for you to do, remember my meditation practice. I started out slowly and built up to daily.

## Physical

- ☐ Stretch and consciously take deep breaths during the day.
- ☐ If you enjoy a good soak in the tub, use Epsom salt or oils to help soothe your body, so you can relax, release, and heal.

## Emotional

- ☐ If you want background music, select something that is relaxing and lifts your spirits.
- ☐ If you like aromatic oils or incense, use them to enhance your environment.

## Mental

- ☐ Sit quietly and **notice your thoughts.**
  - ° Start releasing attachments to what "it" (Ego) wants.
  - ° Shift into spirit and connect with your higher power.
  - ° Listen to your **gentle inner voice** and the guidance you are being given from your spirit.
  - ° Journal or just have a pad where you can jot down any insight that comes through for you.
  - ° Slowly return to the here and now feeling more relaxed and peaceful.
  - ° Thank yourself for taking the time. You can't have a bad attitude if you're in gratitude.
  - ° Drinking water after you relax helps flush the system. Honor your body; it's your temple.

° No judgments or over-analyzing is needed. If your thinking is clearer, that's fine, if you're more relaxed, that's fine too. You accomplished your outcome, to relax a bit and be gentle with yourself. Bravo!

You have just started creating a new healthy habit. It takes twenty-one consecutive days to make or break a habit. The more you practice, the easier it becomes until ES Thinking is your default, and you become your own best support/coach from a place of spirit with unconditional love and balance.

Below is a collection of different tools, all of which support ES Thinking. They have assisted me in processing and moving through challenging situations. I invite you to create your own toolbox of strategies.

**Breath**

The first step in connecting with the flow of energy in our bodies is by becoming aware of our breath.

Never underestimate the power of connecting with your breath. If you noticed in many of the stories I have shared, the moment I connected with my spirit, I began by taking a deep breath or many deep breaths. Breathing helps bring us fully into our body and gives us energy, which is critical for experiencing the Now moment. In that Now moment, we are connecting to the breath of life, to our spirit.

**Journaling**

I have been journaling since I was ten years old. Over the years, my journaling has started and stopped, but it was an integral part in my learning how to connect with my thoughts and feelings. For some reason, I can just let go and put on paper what is going on without my ego interfering. It is the one place where I am completely in my free zone. I have consciously given myself permission to write anything and everything I think and feel without any criticism or judgment about what ends up on the paper. It became a way for me to pull out what was happening in my world when I could not talk about it. Both my ego and spirit are present when I am journaling, and it is a gentle teaching tool I use to identify ego versus spirit thoughts. I typically do not worry about full sentences, punctuation, or whether or not it makes sense. For a period of time, I would write in my dominant right hand and then let the little girl in me write back using my left hand. What I learned was amazing. Some of my writings were neat, and some were what I called my rants and were barely recognizable. If I was ever concerned that someone would read what I wrote and try to have me committed or that someone I wrote about would see it, I would rip it up after I finished and release it as I was ripping it. Sometimes, I would burn it as well as a form of release. The bottom line is that there is no one way to journal. It can be whatever you want it to be.

**Talk Out Loud**

I've shared that I tend to process information verbally. When something is going on, I may talk about it out loud to myself or to God. Sometimes, I would be in my car, cleaning my house, or out walking my dog. The key here is I was alone and needed a way to bring my thoughts and feelings out in the open and bypass my ego that was trying to keep me silent. It helps me to recognize what I am thinking and feeling and when illusions are leading me astray.

## Physical Movement

Sometimes we are stuck, and physical movement is one way to help getting your flow of energy moving again. Any kind of movement can help—cleaning, walking, running, dancing, cycling, boxing, even laughing, etc., whatever is your preference.

## Nature

Being in nature for some can also be healing. Because everything is made up of energy, nature is a place where you can experience more positive energy exchanges. Some people feel closer to their spirit in the presence of nature. I love to walk in nature and find it helps to ground me in the moment where I can fully feel my body and slow down my thoughts. Grounding connects us energetically to the earth. It allows us to be more authentically in our body and receive nourishing energy. By doing this, I feel my emotions and connect with the flow of energy moving through my body. It is much easier to release any thoughts and feelings that are not serving me through that flow of energy.

You can try what's called Grounding, or Earthing. Go barefoot outside for at least a half-hour if possible. Sit, stand, lie, or walk on grass, sand, dirt, or plain concrete. These are conductive surfaces for the body to draw healing energy from the earth.

Grounding improves sleep, blood circulation, and recovery as well as reduces stress to name a few.

## Positive Affirmations/Mantras

This is a vital practice responsible for HUGE shifts since incorporating it into my healing journey. When I am in my critical and judgment zone, I use my thoughts, feelings, and actions to gather information regarding what is blocking me. I then think of an affirmation or mantra that supports me to move into my free zone. I've used statements like: "I am safe; I am releasing any and all fear held within my mind and body; I am pure love; I breathe in love and breathe out any negativity." Some of my favorite mantras have been: "Om namah shivaya" to honor the God within me; and "Nam Myoho Renge Kyo" believing in my unlimited potential.

Earlier I spoke of Louise Hay. In the back of her book, *You Can Heal Your Life*, she gives a list of conditions that we humans can suffer from. She gives the probable thought pattern that can cause each condition and a new thought pattern or affirmation to say to shift your focus from ego to spirit thinking. I went through the entire list and wrote down every condition I had and what new thought pattern would help it. I then used the voice recorder on my phone to record myself listing each and what affirmation I needed to focus on. I left time between each one to be able to repeat it. Every day for months while I walked my dog, I would listen to the recording. Doing so would shift the energy flow moving through my body and really assisted me in getting this habit into my muscle memory. Over time, I found it easier to come up with positive affirmations when I found myself in the critical and judgment zone.

Florence Scovel Shinn was an illustrator and author in the early 1920s whose work, *Your Word is Your Wand*, is also a testament of the power of affirmations. Affirmations and mantras support the statement of "How we think has an impact on how we feel, and how we feel drives our behavior." It supports how there is definitely a mind/body connection.

**Mala Beads**

A mala is simply a string of beads that is used in a meditation practice. Rooted in Hinduism and Buddhism, it is a tool to help you count mantras or positive affirmations. One belief is there are 108 energy centers in our body, and saying a mantra or affirmation 108 times aligns the flow of energy in our bodies with what we are saying.

You may find bracelets and decorative necklaces with fifty-four or twenty-seven beads, half and a quarter of the 108 respectively. This is similar to the concept of rosary and other prayer beads. The way I use them is to get in a comfortable position and choose an affirmation or mantra that resonates with me. I hold the mala in one hand, and as I hold the first bead, I say my affirmation or mantra. As my fingers move onto the next bead, I repeat my saying either out loud or silently in my head. I keep going until I have moved through all 108 beads. What an energy shifter, and it doesn't take that long at all!

**YouTube**

YouTube has a wealth of free videos that can help assist us in ways to accelerate our healing process. There are many guided meditations and positive affirmation videos that can help you quiet your mind and connect with your spirit and higher power. My cousin and I are always sharing new videos with each other on a variety of topics. Sometimes when one resonates with me, it has the opposite effect on her and vice versa. The point is that we are individuals, and you should only take what feels right within you and leave the rest. For any meditation video, I always listen to it first from start to finish to make sure I am comfortable with all that is said before I go into the actual meditation. I also use videos of sound healing, Tibetan bowls and chimes, as background music while I'm relaxing, cleaning, journaling, or writing. I look for titles that support releasing and healing. I play some of them as I sleep. Some of my favorites are Abraham Hicks, Lorie Ladd, Solfeggio Frequency videos, and Lisa Beachy guided meditations.

Sometimes healing between you and another person is needed, but you are unable to make that happen in a face-to-face interaction. Below are two practices I have done that have made a difference in my healing. When we take the time to identify, validate, and release thoughts, emotions, or experiences, there is a ripple effect to those around us.

**Write a Letter to a Person or Situation**

I had an amazing reading once with Elizabeth April. She refers to herself as a Millennial Psychic and Truth Seeker. She is another beautiful soul who helped influence my healing in a game-changer kind of way. During my reading, she instructed me to write a letter answering four questions to help remove a block I was holding onto. This exercise was so healing for me in letting go of emotions from my past that I have given it to many friends and clients and have done it with many other people and situations to help release whatever I needed at the time. The questions are:

~ What were the dynamics of our relationship?
~ Were there any traumas or issues between us?
~ What were my main emotions during that period?
~ What is the conversation I never got to say?

Once your letter is written, write down a list of forgiveness statements. Start with "I forgive..." and fill it in until you feel done. Then take the entire letter and rip it up into little pieces, releasing whatever was written. Then burn it. As you watch the smoke rise up and dissipate, imagine any residue from this person or situation, rising up and dissipating from your energetic field. I have done this exercise in one sitting and spread out over days. This is your process. Honor whatever way works for you.

**Ho'oponopono Prayer**

This is a powerful Hawaiian prayer. Maybe you have heard of how a Hawaiian therapist cured an entire ward of criminally insane patients without ever meeting them or spending any time in the same room with them. The therapist was Dr. Ihaleakala Hew Len. He reviewed each of the patients' files, and then he healed them by healing himself through this prayer. Remember, everything is energy. Our thoughts are energy, and using our thoughts combined with emotion and intention creates an energy exchange that can have a profound positive affect on others. There are four simple steps to this prayer: Repentance, Forgiveness, Gratitude, and Love. The order is not important but using these forces together have an amazing power to heal.

The best part of Ho'oponopono is you don't need anyone else to be there, and you don't need anyone to hear you say the prayer. You can say the words in your head. The power is in the feeling and intention that is put out into the Universe to forgive and love when you say each line of the prayer. The prayer is as follows:

**I'm sorry** (for any part of me that is responsible for this energy or situation)
**Please forgive me** (for any thought, feeling, action of

SUSAN KREBS

mine that contributed to it)

**Thank you** (name anything you are grateful for whether related to issue or not)

**I love you** (say it to yourself, your body, house, God, air, the person you are thinking about, anything or one you can think of)

I used this repeatedly for different relationships and situations that I felt powerless over, and I was blown away by the shifts in me, which rippled out to those it was about. I encourage you to research this in more detail and see for yourself.

**Other**

This is for you to think of one, two, or three tools you have utilized that have helped you manage and move through challenging situations. Think in terms of what you do that helps you quiet your racing mind and tune into your thoughts and feelings. How does using this tool make you feel, and how does it affect your body?

∞

**Exploration:**

The following are questions Lorie Ladd came up with, and they parallel the concepts of ES Thinking:

Think of a situation that is upsetting to you and bring yourself into the Now moment. Ask yourself the following questions:

☐ What are my thoughts?

_____

_____

_____

☐ What am I feeling?

_____

_____

_____

☐ What is my body doing?

_____

_____

_____

For the next two questions, remember to stay in the free zone!

☐ Where am I? Am I staying in the experience or escaping?

_____

_____

_____

☐ How present am I getting with this experience and feeling it all the way through?

_____

_____

_____

Stay in the experience as much as possible whenever it is possible to do so. Be gentle with yourself and let it be okay to be wherever you are at in the process.

"Be not afraid of growing slowly.
Be afraid only of standing still."

~Unknown

It is important to remember that different experiences have different levels of discomfort. The more uncomfortable the energy (such as trauma and abuse), the longer it will take to process through. An altercation with someone at work will not likely take as long as someone working through an abusive relationship.

Some may have experiences to move through that need the help of an outside source, especially if you are going through more dense uncomfortable energetic issues. It could show up in an eye-opening conversation with a friend or by working with a life coach, counselor, therapist, or energy healer. Listen to your spirit. It is very freeing and empowering to access the resources of someone who is trained in helping a person move through these types of experiences. If you set the intention of asking for and receiving help, your spirit will lead you to the right source. Look for the signs, and they will come.

A saying I have adopted from Lorie Ladd is that through each experience I am processing through, I am becoming the next higher version of myself. In my journey of self-discovery, I realized that I am a perfectionist, and I want to get to the positive end result—like yesterday! SO not real! By understanding that life will always have challenges, I resonate with my healing journey taking me to the next higher version of myself. There is no perfect version. It is ever changing, and there is always more to learn.

ES thinking is an integral part of feeling yourself through a challenge. By connecting to your thoughts and feelings, you experience an opportunity to look at, listen to, and feel what is happening.

~ How much is driven by ego, and how much is driven by spirit?
~ What illusions are you holding onto?
~ How does this experience shift when you are in your free zone connected to spirit?
~ What signs do you notice from your spirit that is guiding you to more understanding and clarity?

The information you receive will help you move through these challenges and process it through to completion with as much ease as possible. That is the gift. That is choosing Love.

# II

## Creating the Balance from Our Heart

"Embrace YOU...Believe in yourself, in this very
moment...forgive yourself for all mistakes and 'bad'
decisions you may have made in the past. Do not allow
other's opinions or judgments of who you were yesterday
or decades ago define who you are today. Each and every
day opens new doors for miracles of healing to occur in our
lives. Embrace these miracles, big or small, even those
you may presently be unaware of. Live in this moment,
for this is all we have. Give thanks to your Higher
Power for all that you are, for the very breath that
allows life, love, and abundance to flow to
you and through you forever more.
Live in the Light of All That IS."

~ Angie Karan

Balance is a word that has different perceptions. Some think of balance as a scale of 50/50 or an even distribution of something. We are not talking about being in our ego state 50 percent of the time and spirit state the other 50 percent of the time. By reflecting on different situations that occur in our daily lives, we gather information of when we are in our ego state or spirit state, and what worked for us and what didn't. It all starts with being more present in the moment. Being in the Now, we are able to use the information gathered and move back and forth between our ego and spirit states more effectively. This supports us being in balance and obtaining our desired results with more ease and grace.

Many people in our society today spend much of their time in their ego states. Learning about and recognizing our ego-driven thoughts helps develop our relationship with our spirit. This awareness becomes the gateway into entering the zone of ES Thinking, a blending of the two working in more harmony.

We have been talking all along about how our thoughts trigger our emotions and our emotions trigger our behaviors, right? The balance part occurs when we recognize when our thoughts are being driven by ego, which triggers our feelings, negative or positive. When we catch ourselves especially in a negative state, we can choose to use our new skills and consciously connect with our spirit to achieve a more desired, favorable result. It's also important to notice when we're in a positive ego-thinking state. We want to validate all those thoughts and feelings no matter what they are. When we validate without judgment, we create the balance that supports them being in harmony and working together. Spirit only wants what's for our highest good. Spirit is total acceptance and love.

ES Thinking moves you through difficult human experiences, assisting you in becoming more aware and present as to what is happening physically, emotionally, and mentally.

When using the six steps of ES Thinking, you will be guided and supported to move through experiences to completion. That's when the new higher version of yourself emerges with gratitude. The unique part is that they don't have to be used in a sequential order. Consider the steps as tools and trust your spirit will connect you with the right tools for each situation. You can use one, two, or all, depending on the situation and how you respond. You'll know.

1. To start the process, become present. In this moment, identify what is happening to you physically, emotionally, and mentally.

2. Use whatever tools you feel will support your process (See Chapter 10).

3. Recognize the positive intent of ego-driven thoughts and illusions. Identify any emotions and old beliefs that surface and may not be true or that no longer serve you.

4. Move into your free zone by releasing any criticism and judgment, and go to that impartial/neutral position of spirit.

5. Connect to your spirit and experience the highest form of love of self and others. Listen to the guidance being given. Ask yourself: *What do I want now?*

6. Be grateful for all parts of the experience (good, bad, and ugly!). Take the information learned and put it in your toolbox. Now, move forward with more ease and grace as this new higher version of yourself.

Below is an example of how I processed a challenging relationship through to completion utilizing the tools above:

I knew a person for years and considered this person a friend. We did not talk all the time, and by letting life get in the way, we had started to grow apart. I always considered her the type of friend that, no matter how much time went by, we always picked right up where we left off. Unbeknownst to me, she felt like I had betrayed her and was hurt. I found out how she was feeling by hearing that she was talking about me negatively and even involved social media to vent her perceived hurt. I was clueless! When I found out, I was deeply hurt. It always bothered me when someone did not like me, but it is especially difficult when that someone was my friend and knew the kind of person I am. I tried reaching out to her to work it out, but she was not in a place to want to do that.

Let me share with you the impact this had on my Physical, Mental, and Emotional state.

~ I felt physically ill. My stomach was tied up in knots. I had trouble sleeping, and my body felt restless, which made it difficult to focus. I was processing through my **Physical body.**

~ I observed my thoughts. Some of them were: *How could she do that to me? How could she think that? I don't un-*

*derstand. She knows me better than that. How could she in-volve all those other people?* Of course, I was angry as well, so some of my thoughts were pretty derogatory to-ward her. Then, I recognized my thoughts about me. *I thought I could trust her. I should never have opened myself up to her the way I did.* I was processing it through my **Mental body.**

~  By observing my thoughts, I recognized how I was feeling. I was angry, embarrassed, shocked, hurt, scared, and I felt vulnerable to an attack. I was proc-essing it through my **Emotional body**. I noticed how those emotions were driving my behavior. I felt I had to defend myself and was making sure anyone who knew of this heard my side of the story. I pulled back from other relationships because the situation trig-gered my need to protect myself. I started feeling that I could not trust people, and I avoided conversations with them. I was on guard and no longer felt safe in that circle of friends. I started turning toward ways to dissociate (eating crap, smoking, and sleeping).

Keep in mind, all the above was happening simultane-ously. This was a pretty intense time for me. When my mind went off on different tangents, I consciously took deep breaths, connecting to my body and spirit in a safe way. Sometimes, I would just breathe in and out until I felt more grounded and calmer. In this state, I was able to step back and observe my thoughts and feelings without being encased by them.

I was guided by my spirit to use different tools to help me process it through. Meditating and connecting with my higher power helped me. I shared all my thoughts and feelings with God. I was guided to journal, reach out to certain people, and use them as my support system. I used mantras and affirmations, took walks, and eventually used the Ho'oponopono Prayer since my friend did not want to talk to me about the situation.

As I observed my thoughts, I recognized I was completely in my ego state, feeling anger, judgment, fear, and pain. The positive intent of my ego was to avoid further pain and move away from all those upsetting feelings. I was back in survival mode.

I took walks to connect more with my body in the moment, so I would dissociate less. By bringing all these thoughts and feelings to the surface, I recognized how critical of her and myself I was being. I explored what belief systems they were stemming from, and I questioned whether they were illusions. I used mantras and positive affirmations to reinforce my new belief systems. This part took some time to process through.

My spirit was helping me connect with support systems. I connected with people who helped me recognize that certain shifts were happening. I began thinking how she had her perception of what occurred, and I had mine. I took out "who's right and wrong" from the equation and looked at it from more of an observation place in my free zone. I stayed present to my thoughts and actively engaged my spirit to create a shift.

Here are a few examples of how my thinking shifted with the help of my spirit:

~ *How could she do this to me?* Became:

*She thinks I betrayed her and is reacting in a way that works for her. For some reason, she needs to tell people and put stuff out on social media to make herself feel better in some way.*

My spirit guided me toward my free zone, and I took myself out of it and focused in on what she thinks and feels. I realized that her actions were a reflection of her relationship with herself and what she needed.

~ *How could she think that?* Became:

*She is basing her belief on her model of the world. Hers is different than mine. She is not thinking of me; she is thinking of herself and how she feels.*

~ *I don't understand.* Became:

*I may never understand fully. Bottom line, she felt hurt and reacted. There are so many things different people do and say (not just her) that I do not understand.*

I had to let some of this go. My spirit guided me toward people who helped me shift inward, so I could focus on myself and what I needed to understand to move on.

~ *How could she involve all these other people?* Became:

*I am a private person in general and look to keep things in. She is the opposite. Because I am so private, her behavior trig-*

*gered many layers of old belief systems that made me want to crawl back into a shell and hide.*

I had to go in my free zone **continually** here because this was a weak spot for me.

~ *Why wouldn't she just come to me?* Became:

*I have no clue to this day why she wouldn't, and I have just had to let that one go. It is not the way I would have handled the situation.*

It gave me more information of what is important to me in a friendship though.

~ *She knows me better than that.* Became:

*Well, she is viewing me and our friendship through her own lens of the world. Mine looked way different. Maybe she did not know me the way I thought she did. And that's okay!*

~ *I thought I could trust her.* Became:

*I can trust myself always! I am not responsible for the way she reacts. She is not responsible for the way I react.*

I began looking at ways I can react differently for my own peace of mind.

~ *I should never have opened myself up to her the way I did.* Became:

*But then I would have never had the beautiful moments that made up parts of our friendship. I truly am grateful for those laughs and camaraderie we once shared.*

This is what the Ho'oponopono prayer helped me to understand.

This whole situation gave me an opportunity to explore my own beliefs and thoughts. Instead of focusing outward on the other person or situation, I was able to go inward and learn many things about myself and what is important to me. I was able to enter my free zone and see this person as another human who was hurting and reacting in a way that was based on her own beliefs and model of the world.

How do I know I processed this situation through to completion? Because I no longer have a negative physical, mental, or emotional reaction when I think of her. Do I wish she would have come to me so we could have had the opportunity to work it out? YES! But she didn't. I bless her and am grateful for the good parts we had. I have healed and released the parts that no longer serve me. It is a very liberating feeling.

ES Thinking is a process and takes time to integrate. Just keep practicing until it becomes a part of your muscle memory. The more you practice, the easier it gets!

"For those who are willing to make an effort,
great miracles and wonderful treasures
are in store"

~Isaac Bashevis Singer

Every moment of every day, we are always moving toward or away from something. At times, your experiences may be going smoothly, but often, you may feel stuck or sense that something is not working. What you want in life is not being manifested. You don't understand why your life is not happening in the way you want it to but are not sure what to do about it. All that you need to understand is that in this situation, your amazing ego and mind are in the driver's seat. Your ego and mind are in control. Become aware of this. Recognize it for what it is without judging or criticizing it. Then, remember that we all have this higher power/spirit that wants to move us through it. Your spirit always wants to lead you in the direction of what is in your highest good.

As you are learning to shift into your connection to spirit, the more self-love and acceptance you will experience. The more receptive you are to the highest form of unconditional love, the more you learn how to receive and give it, the more you live it.

I am encouraging you, as you go through your day, to challenge yourself to be present. Put a sticky note on your fridge, bathroom mirror, desk at work, and in your car with this question on it. "How present can I be right now?" Then when you see it, check in with how your body feels, what thoughts you are thinking, and what emotions you are feeling right now. Ask yourself, "Am I in my free zone? What is my spirit saying to me? What am I grateful for?"

This is the beginning of deepening your relationship with loving yourself. You are an incredibly beautiful being of light that is ready to move forward on your path in this crazy world we live in. There **is** a light at the end of the tunnel; there **is** a silver lining; it **is** possible to manage life's challenges with more ease and grace from a place of love. I promise you! This is a journey of self-discovery that is uniquely yours. You really do deserve it! Let the journey begin in gratitude with ES Thinking.

**The light in me honors the light in you!**

# A Prayer for You

God grant me the Grace of Reverence for my life,
that I may be grateful that I am alive.

God grant me the Grace of Piety,
that I may see every human being as divine.

God grant me the Grace of Understanding,
that I may see beauty and truth in my relationships
with others.

God grant me the Grace of Fortitude,
that I may have courage when you call my name.

God grant me the Grace of Counsel,
that I may hear you when you guide me.

God grant me the Grace of Knowledge,
that I may understand the higher meaning of things.

God grant me the Grace of Wisdom,
that I may see clearly the choices I need to make.

Let nothing, Dear God, disturb the silence of the
peace in my heart with you.

Amen

*Caroline Myss, a renowned author on healing shared this prayer in a
video on the Seven Graces in her book, Defy Gravity. I read this often.
It sums up all my hopes and prayers for you.
Feel free to tear out this page.*

# About the Author

Susan is a certified Practitioner of Neuro-Linguistic Programming (NLP) and supports the Princeton Center for NLP as an assistant trainer and a helping professional advisor.

She is the co-founder, along with Mary Demetria Davis, of the practice of ES Thinking.

As a successful licensed Speech Pathologist, she has over twenty years of experience working with children with multiple handicaps and learning disabilities.

Susan is known for her compassion and skill in improving physical communication issues and brings a unique perspective to applications of NLP for adults and children.

She is a well-respected member of several Speech/ Language and Hearing Associations in New York and holds a Masters Degree of Science in Communication Disorders.

# Notes

Hay, Louise: *You Can Heal Your Life* (Carlsbad: Hay House Inc., 1999)

Myss, Caroline: *Defy Gravity: Healing Beyond the Bounds of Reason* (Carlsbad: Hay House Inc., 2009)

Scovel Shinn, Florence: *Your Word is Your Wand* ( n.p.: Sublime Books, 2014)

Tolle, Eckhart: *The Power of Now: A Guide to Spiritual Enlightenment* (Novato: Namaste Publishing and New World Library, 1999)